FOR THE LEAST OF THESE

CHILDREN OF NEGLECT. STORIES OF HOPE.

21stCENTURY
P R E S S
READING YOU LOUD AND CLEAR.

For the Least of These

Published by 21st Century Press
Springfield, Missouri U.S.A.
Printed in U.S.A.

21st Century Press is an evangelical Christian publisher dedicated to serving the local church with purpose books. We believe God's vision for 21st Century Press is to provide church leaders with biblical, user-friendly materials that will help them evangelize, disciple and minister to children, youth and families.

21st Century Press
2131 W. Republic Rd.
PMB 41
Springfield, MO 65807
800-658-0284
www.21stcenturypress.com

Cover Design: Keith Locke
Book Design & Illustrations: Zach Dyer

ISBN 978-0-9817769-7-2

dedication

I am profoundly grateful to my Heavenly Father for holding my hand through every experience written in these pages. He is also wholly responsible for piecing every part of this book perfectly into place.

To my unbelievably supportive and loving parents: I could never come up with enough words to express my appreciation to you. I have been so blessed to witness the amazing examples of sacrificial love, undeserved blessings, and whole-hearted obedience to God that you two have portrayed throughout my life. I have attempted to pattern my life after yours, Dad and Mom. I have tried to be to the children that God has placed in my path, all the things that you have been to me. You both continue to amaze me. When I count my blessings, being your daughter is at the top of the list.

donate

The Precious Miracles Foundation is financially supported by donations from individuals, families, and churches. We rely solely on the gifts of our supporters to provide food, clothing, medical care, education, and therapies for the children in our care. To find out more about how you can be a part of our support team please visit our website at www.preciousmiracles.org.

We are proud to be able to say that 100% of every dollar given to Precious Miracles is used to directly support the ministry in Ecuador.

Table of Contents

introduction

When I named my organization several years ago, I was not aware that I would see and experience God's supernatural intervention so frequently. In the years that followed the foundation's beginning, my life would be overwhelmed by precious little miracles. This is the story of some of them.

In September 2000, I went to Ecuador to start a home for abandoned children. My goal never was to open an orphanage but rather a home. The main problem I witnessed at the already existing orphanages in the Quito area was the uneven ratio of swarms of children to few caregivers. I chose not to take in a limitless number of children. I established a maximum capacity of 10 that later turned to 15. We maintained a 5:1 child to staff ratio around the clock. The children who were able to speak called me 'Mommy' and their caregivers 'Tia'. Our home would resemble a family in every way possible. For a little over four years of our home's operation, I lived directly on the premises. Then for the remaining three years I lived in an apartment and would spend only the days at the home.

The other major difference between our home and an orphanage was the desire to transition each child as soon as possible to his or her permanent family. We did not wish to raise the children until adulthood. Some of the children were returned back to their families of origin when the crisis that brought them to our doors was solved, and others were united with an adoptive family. Some children were adopted in the country of Ecuador and some left to the U.S. or Europe.

The last major distinction between Precious Miracles and other orphanages in Ecuador was our willingness to take in the children with special needs. There are only two homes in the Quito area that will take in abandoned or orphaned children that suffer from some form of disability. Of the forty children that were cared for in the seven years, 18 of them were diagnosed with some type of special need. Precious Miracles was approved by the government of Ecuador as a non-profit organization in April of 2002, and I was named the Executive Director and President of the Foundation.

The definition of the word precious according to Webster's Collegiate Dictionary is: Priceless, beloved, cherished, darling, of great desirability, excessively refined. The meaning of the word miracles is: Amazing, remarkable, an extraordinary event manifesting a supernatural act of God. The name I chose for this home was most assuredly not a mistake.

Every child is precious in our Father's eyes; the child with two parents, the child who has been thrown away by his parents, the child who is healthy and thriving, the child who is disabled, the child who is loved and the child who is difficult to love. Every child is priceless, beloved, and of great value to our Lord.

The way in which each child arrived to our home and into our lives can only be described as miraculous. It was God's doing. The transformation that we witnessed with every one of the children was phenomenal. What each one survived, endured and tolerated is remarkable.

This book has my tears woven into every page. The seven years of my life, consumed and defined by Precious Miracles was a trying and emotional time, and writing this book was a heartrending task. I wanted people to hear these stories. I wanted people to know about the hurt and pain that goes on in the world and how God gives beauty for ashes.

God works miracles on a regular basis, and I have been fortunate to have witnessed so many of them. The children of Precious Miracles taught me many life lessons, and I wanted to share them.

The stories you are about to read are personal and very private. I have changed the names of several of the children, their birth parents, and their adoptive parents in an attempt to protect privacy. I have always believed that a past that has no place in a person's memory should only be told when necessary and with the utmost sensitivity.

Some of you may know some of the children in this book personally. And it's to you that I plead, do not see this book as a mystery to be solved. I ask that you not try to figure out which child is which. I have been an eyewitness to God's amazing grace, power, and awesome sovereignty. My goal in the composition of this book was to share those blessings with others and to give God the glory. My life has been forever changed by the smallest, the orphaned and the abandoned.

1

Catie

A Dream Come True

"Stacey, do you think you could take another child for us?" I recognized the voice on the phone. It was Melinda, the Director of 'For His Children.' Theirs was an organization similar to what I had planned on establishing. Melinda and her husband, Clark were also American missionaries living in Ecuador who had begun a home for abandoned children. "I know you haven't gotten the government's approval yet," she continued. I turned and looked at 5 month old Paula blissfully moving back and forth in her swing.

We had been flying a bit under the radar with Paula. Because Precious Miracles had not been approved by the Ecuadorian government to operate as a foundation yet, I was technically not allowed to receive children in my home. But I had agreed to be a foster mother to Paula for "For His Children" and by doing so was not breaking any laws. "We have a little girl that needs some more one on one attention than we can give her," continued Melinda. "Catie is a child with special needs. She has cleft lip and palate."

Not knowing what that was but not wanting to sound ignorant, I readily agreed. I told Melinda I'd be at her place the next afternoon to meet little Catie, spend some time with her and then bring her home.

"I can do this," I convinced myself after hanging up the

phone. "I can take care of two baby girls." In the months prior, I had started to interview women for the Precious Miracles' staff, assuring them that as soon as the foundation was approved, I would call them. Just this week I had gone ahead with the training and orientation of a few of the ladies. It was an absolute act of faith, since I had received no indication that Precious Miracles was near its approval. After all, it had been 18 months since I had first submitted the paperwork. Wanting to be ready when the time came, however, I had requested that the ladies come to their day of training. The other half of the women would be here tomorrow to receive their orientation.

I planned my day out in my head. I would train the second group of women, drop Paula off at my mom's and then go pick up Catie. It was all falling perfectly into place. I figured I would proceed with hiring a couple ladies to trade off helping me during the day with my two girls. By nature I am a planner and extremely organized. I could not have planned the sequence of events more perfectly. I thought to myself, "God really is amazing!"

The next day went as planned. I had a successful training in the morning and then put together a diaper bag for Paula. I wanted to be able to devote all my attention to Catie while at For His Children, so I left Paula with her favorite baby-sitter. When I arrived at my parents' house, my dad was waiting at the door with a big smile on his face.

"I have news for you," he said.

"What Dad? What is it?"

"On the 23rd of April, Precious Miracles received the final signature," he said. "You're approved!"

Eighteen months after submitting the papers requesting permission to run a home for abandoned children, and finally the day arrived where I had received the official acceptance. What a day today was turning out to be! My parents and I hugged and sniffled a bit, our eyes wet with emotion. It was finally happening. My dreams were coming true. I had a precious little girl who had stolen my heart, my second little girl was moments away from joining my family, and I had finally received the permission to help so many more children. I had no idea how many children it would be or how God was about to bless me.

With a big smile, I drove across town to For His Children to meet Catie. I was welcomed warmly by the staff there, and then led to her room. She was laying face down when I walked in. I was not prepared for what I was about to see when she turned around. The caregiver scooped her up and handed her to me and I caught my breath. This miniscule little baby had only one nostril. The rest of her nose and the left side of her lip were completely missing. Where her facial features should be, was just one gaping hole. She looked up at me and I looked down in her face and smiled. "Hi sweet baby," I said. The caregiver sensing my discomfort patiently explained Catie's condition to me.

"We have to feed her milk using a medicine dropper," she explained. Catie was eight weeks old and weighed seven pounds. "When she is 10 weeks old, if she weighs 10 pounds, they will do her first surgery to close up her mouth and fix her nose," continued the caregiver. I held little Catie in my arms and rocked her back and forth.

"I'll do my best," I whispered. "I'm not sure if I'm the best person to take care of you, but I can promise you that I'll try my hardest." I took Catie home and shortly afterward, my parents joined me with Paula. "I don't know if I can do this Mom!" I said. "I'm not sure I can handle two."

My parents prayed with me, and we thanked God for the new miracle that had arrived in my home. This became a tradition with every child following Catie. After praying they hugged me tightly and assured me that with God's help, I did have the strength to complete the task in front of me, and then they were gone. I was alone with my two-month old and my five-month old.

Feeding Catie did prove to be a very difficult task. By the time she got hungry, I could not get the milk in her little tummy fast enough to calm the hunger pangs. She would cry harder and this would only make it more complicated for her to swallow the milk. I tried to be patient and keep at it. But she was crying harder and harder by the second and the milk was coming out her nostril. Soon, I too was crying.

"Sweet baby, please stop." I cried. "I'm doing the best that I can. I need you to calm down because we're getting nowhere!"

Catie looked up at me, and then as if she had understood my words, took a deep breath and stopped crying. I squeezed the milk in the medicine dropper again and tried once more. Soon I had the rhythm down, and she was feeling her tummy fill up. After almost an hour, she had her fill and was asleep in my arms. I leaned back in my chair and sighed. I closed my eyes and let my tense shoulders drop. As soon as I did, Paula who had been quietly sitting in a bouncy chair started to fuss.

"Oh my goodness," I said out loud. "I truly am not capable of this. I can't. I just can't." I laid Catie down in the playpen and went to pick up Paula. "Are you hungry?" I asked.

"Thanks for waiting to be hungry until your sister was done," I smiled at her. She smiled back.

I didn't get much sleep for the first few nights. I had help during the days, but I'd be alone at night. Admitting my limitations, I proceeded to hire staff for the nights as well.

As soon as I did, more children joined us. Our house was filling up rapidly. We would weigh Catie every day to see if she had gained an ounce. I knew that if her 10 week marker came around and she was not weighing the required 10 pounds, the surgeon would postpone the operation. "Please get fat," I would tell her. It remained so difficult to feed her, and I was sure that she was burning up the calories as they entered her body because she would get so upset and aggravated.

The day of her surgery was fast approaching, and I took Catie to the pediatrician, Dr. Castillo. "Please weigh her first," I asked him. He obliged and she weighed 9.35 pounds. That was close enough!

Catie's operation was performed on the scheduled date in the doctor's office. I was surprised that it was not being done in a hospital operating room. It was also much quicker than I had anticipated. She came out with her little face covered in bandages, and it was an upsetting sight for me. For the first week after her surgery, one staff member had to hold Catie constantly. She was only able to breathe out of her mouth, and this was not natural for her. Whether she was awake or asleep, she was in someone's arms so we could make sure to keep her little mouth open.

Catie's recovery was difficult for all of us. It was very complicated for her to eat with the bandages covering her little face. We had to wrap her arms at her sides so she would not pull on or rip the bandages off. She was in a constant state of discomfort. One night as I was headed to bed, one of the caregivers came crying up the stairs. Catie was covered in blood. I rushed her to the nearest hospital. Some of her stitches had come loose, causing her mouth to hemorrhage. In less than an hour I was home again with a very tired little baby.

Catie continued to grow and thrive and develop into a healthy, well-adjusted baby. The day arrived in which I received the news that a family was ready to adopt their little girl. When Catie's parents arrived at Precious Miracles, they were awe-struck by their beautiful, bouncing baby girl. Catie would join an older sister who was thrilled and enamored with her new playmate. After spending some time getting to know each other, Catie's mother turned to me and said, "We heard that you still have contact with Catie's birth mother. Is that true?"

"Yes," I answered.

"We would like to meet her. We think it's important when Catie is older and asks about her history, that we have as much information as possible to give to her."

"I'll arrange it right away," I assured them.

Meredith was surprised at my phone call. "It has been a long time," she started.

"Yes, Meredith, I know it has," I said, trying to maintain the calmness of my voice. The last time I had seen Meredith had been at her visit to my home. She had made three visits to see her daughter. On one occasion she asked me why I had started this foundation.

"What makes you love children that aren't your own?" she had asked. I took the opportunity to share God's love for us in sending us His Son. I explained to her that it was God's love through me that I had for these children. We prayed together and I gave her a Bible. I smiled at the beautiful memory of how God used Precious Miracles as a way for me to testify to His love.

"But sanctify the Lord God in your hearts, and always be ready to give a defense to everyone who asks you a reason for the hope that is in you" (1 Peter 3:15).

"How is Catie?" Meredith asked, returning my thoughts to the present.

"Catie is doing wonderfully, and I'm calling to let you know that her adoptive family is here in Ecuador and they requested meeting you. Are you up for that?"

There was a long pause and then Meredith said, "Totally! I'd love to see my baby's new family."

The afternoon arrived in which Catie's two families would meet. Catie was awake and happily sitting on her new mother's lap. The proud family sat side by side on the couch.

I was seated in a chair nearby. Meredith entered the room,

and I could feel the tension. She remained calm and poised as she saw her baby in the arms of another woman. They talked for a while. Meredith explained her situation and her reasons for choosing another life for her daughter. Catie's adoptive parents described the country they lived in and the life they led with their older daughter. I sat quietly in the chair fighting to keep my emotions controlled.

"This is what it's all about," I thought peacefully. This is the cycle I wanted to see when I dreamed up this foundation. What a beautiful thing to take a child with a grim future and turn that life around. To be able to give a family the joy of having a child when they are no longer able to do so biologically was an added bonus. The greatest joy of all was to know that one more person was on her way to heaven because of the work of Precious Miracles. "I could quit now," I thought, "and everything would be a success."

I led our small group in prayer. I prayed for Meredith as she was saying her final good byes to her daughter. I prayed for Catie and her new family as they embarked on their new journey together. Then, photos were taken and hugs were exchanged and soon that momentous day had concluded. Meredith went on her way. I never heard from her again. Catie went with her new family and a few days later, they were on a flight leaving Ecuador. I got back into my car and dabbed my eyes with a tissue. I laughed at the thought I had just had about quitting. I really can't quit now, I thought. I have six children waiting for me at home. And so I drove off towards home and my beautiful family that was waiting for me.

2

alexandra

My Precious Sister

Many people wonder how I decided to start a home for abandoned children in Ecuador. The fact that I went to a third world country at a relatively young age to open an "orphanage" seems to be my most fascinating feature. But the fact is, I did not decide on my own to go to Ecuador. I also did not decide to open Precious Miracles. God made both of those decisions for me. First and foremost, He put the desire in my heart to work with needy children. Then He opened the doors in His perfect timing to make my dream a reality. He guided every step that I took in Ecuador with every child that I cared for.

This was the Lord's doing; it is marvelous in our eyes (Psalm 118:23).

I cannot take credit for the ministry that was done there. God deserves all the praise and the glory. The successes of Precious Miracles were only by His grace. I was privileged to be the one He chose to use as His instrument. It was earnestly not my doing, for it would have been impossible for me to achieve in my own power what God fulfilled through the Precious Miracles Foundation.

There was a sequence of events that brought me to Ecuador,

and I share them to show how perfectly intended every one of our days are in God's plan.

Your eyes have seen my unformed substance; and in Your book were all written the days that were ordained for me, when as yet there was not one of them (Psalm 139:16).

For this part of the story, we will go back in time. I was a happy six-year old girl with curly brown hair, a dimply smile, and a carefree attitude. It was Sunday afternoon. My parents, older brother and I had just returned home from church. With my Sunday school coloring sheet in hand, I climbed the stairs into my toy loft. I carefully lined up all my dolls in neat rows along the wall. Then looking into the expressionless faces before me, I repeated the story I had heard that morning. My mom walked past my room and stopped when she heard my voice, wondering to whom I was talking. She stood quietly at my door listening. When I had finished the story, she said, "Wow Stacey, you have a lot of babies!"

"Oh!" I said startled that she had been listening. I then explained, "They're not MY babies. These are orphans. They don't have mommies, so I take care of them."

A few months later in December, while I was in school, my mom had a plan to clean and fix up my dolls. She took every one of them and "bathed" them, sewed up the clothes that were torn, and made other necessary repairs. On Christmas morning it was her turn to line them all up. They were clean and beautiful and they even smelled nice. She showed me what she had done and then explained that it was her present to my orphanage.

After receiving all my other gifts that morning, I crawled up into her lap and said, "Mom, my favorite present this year was the one you gave my orphanage!"

I believe God gives us glimpses our entire lives of what He

wants from us. These two scenes were previews to what my life would become. Twenty years later, I was still lining up children. These however, did have expressions on their faces and voices emerged from their mouths! And these did not necessarily stay put after I lined them up.

Also twenty years later, my mom was still giving priceless gifts to my orphanage. And every year they were still my favorite presents.

Six years after the doll/ orphanage scene, we find me at age 12 and in the seventh grade. My brother Zac was in the ninth grade. On a dark Friday night, Zac's two best friends, Luis and Cesar, were out witnessing door to door when they were hit and killed by a drunk driver. My brother's life was never the same after that. And although the tragedy affected me in a completely different way, my life was never the same either.

Cesar was a new believer, and before he had come to know Jesus as his Savior, he had fathered a child with his girlfriend Sofia. His daughter, Alexandra, was just two weeks away from her second birthday when he died. Cesar had full custody of Alexandra at the time of his death. Because of this, his family needed help with her care. My mom, always sensitively aware of other's needs, especially when children are involved, quickly offered to help. She had been a stay at home mom all our lives, and she asserted that she had the time to care for Alex during the daytime. This way, Alex's grandparents could continue their own jobs and not pay for day care.

So while Zac and I were at school, Alex was at our house being cared for by Mom. The first day I met her is permanently engraved in my memory. Her head had been shaved, and I thought she had cancer. She was excruciatingly shy and introverted. She stood cowering in a corner looking down at the floor. She was potty trained, and the word "picho," when she needed to use the restroom, was the only word we heard out of her mouth. My mom and I questioned if she had a cognitive disability.

Days turned into weeks, and soon Alex's extended family asked if she could stay a few nights a week at our house. My parents enthusiastically agreed. Those weeks turned into months, and before I knew what had happened, Alex was a permanent member of our family. Having been the baby of the family and the only girl, I was less than thrilled when I discovered our new arrangement. Being a teenager probably didn't help much either. But Alex made it extremely difficult for me to be jealous or mad at her. She was a remarkable little girl. After feeling more secure in our home, she opened up surprisingly.

We discovered not only did she not have a cognitive disability but she was a brilliant little girl. She was sweet, obedient, and entertaining.

We became fast friends. Soon I pleaded with my mom to let Alex sleep in my room. The toy loft that once housed all my dolls was now Alex's bedroom. We were inseparable. I voluntarily took over most of Alex's care giving; bathing her, dressing her, combing out her curly hair, and then even teaching her to write her alphabet. After school I'd race home to play with my little sister. She was the highlight of my days. We would stay up at night talking and giggling. Alex lived in our home for three years before God sent her permanent family. After her adoption was finalized, she moved with her new parents to Kansas. Her loving and thoughtful parents knew the bond that had formed between Alex and our family could not and should not be broken, and they allowed her to remain a part of our lives. We still refer to each other as sisters. If you could see Ali (as she is now known) today, you would remark on her beauty, her intelligence, her sweet and kind spirit, her work ethic, her friendliness and her outstanding smile.

Alex was the first orphan I had ever known, and my heart

was changed because of her. It was through Alex that I realized that when abandonment occurs or parents die, the most innocent of victims are the ones who suffer the greatest. Alex didn't have any say in her life history. She didn't ask to be born into a non-existent home to a teenage mother in poverty. She didn't ask to lose her father. She didn't ask to be brought to our home.

When I number the children of the Precious Miracles Foundation, I should count Alex as the first. She was the first child needing a home, love, and attention, who was brought to my home to have all those needs fulfilled. Alexandra truly was the first Precious Miracle. Alex's presence in my life forever shaped my personality. She is the inspiration for my life's work. She is the instrument God used to open my eyes to the needs of innocent children.

Fast forward five more years. It was a bright, Sunday morning in Lusaka, Zambia. I had been on the continent of Africa for almost two months with my maternal grandparents and had seen and experienced a whole other book of details. I should mention that I had been surrounded by missionaries my whole life. My parents, their friends, two of my uncles, and even my paternal grandparents were missionaries. I even went to a school primarily created for children of missionaries. I probably had more missionary exposure than any other person alive! While in Africa, I had met still more of God's servants whose life experiences encouraged and overwhelmed me. I met couples who at one point in their career had to flee for their lives to avoid the wars in their country. I met missionaries who had withstood incredible persecution and others who dealt with unbelievable family crises. I had seen their great faith in God's provision. I saw their willingness to obey despite the sacrifices they would make and costs they would pay.

On this particular morning, I remember clearly hearing God saying, "This is what I want from you. I want you to serve me like these people have served me. I want you to spread my love to people who have never felt loved. I want you to sacrifice your own desires and wants for the people I will bring across your path."

I had felt God calling me many times before, but had been so afraid to listen. I was fearful that if I said yes to His calling, He would send me somewhere terrible and make me do work I hated. I was so frightened to accept His plan for my life that I pretended I didn't hear Him.

But this day was different. I did not want to escape anymore. He was calling me in a very personal way. I broke down before my Lord and said, "Okay, I give up. I surrender everything. I surrender my reservations and my requests. I surrender my worries and my wishes. I surrender my doubts and my dreams. I choose to serve you for the rest of my life no matter what you ask of me. I choose today to obey and follow you."

As I poured out my deepest fears and my secret hopes, I heard God say gently to me "My child, I know the desires of your heart. I put them there! I gave you a specific love for children because they are who I want you to serve. I gave you Ecuador as your home for many years because that is where I want you to serve me. I know you and love you. I am your Father. I was waiting for you to surrender all your selfish needs and wants because I need ALL of you."

Trust in the Lord with all your heart, and lean not on your own understanding; in all your ways acknowledge Him, and He shall direct your paths (Proverbs 3:5-6).

3

zachary and flor
From Discarded to Cherished

"Then the King will say to those on His right hand, 'Come, you blessed of My Father, inherit the kingdom prepared for you from the foundation of the world: for I was hungry and you gave Me food; I was thirsty and you gave Me drink; I was a stranger and you took Me in; I was naked and you clothed Me; I was sick and you visited Me; I was in prison and you came to Me.' Then the righteous will answer Him saying, 'Lord, when did we see You hungry and feed You, or thirsty and give You drink? When did we see You a stranger and take You in, or naked and clothe You? Or when did we see You sick, or in prison, and come to You?' And the King will answer and say to them 'Assuredly I say to you, inasmuch as you did it to one of the least of these My brethren, you did it to Me'" (Matthew 25: 34- 40).

My call was to the 'least of these.' I knew when I opened my home, that I would be caring for a very specific group of children. Most of them would be infants, the least in size of the human species. They would be abandoned or orphaned children, lacking even the most basic of necessities: the care of a mother. By being abandoned, they would have been deemed the least in importance to even their own flesh and blood.

Many of the children would most likely be suffering from some type of physical, mental, or emotional disability, and by society's standards be considered the least in significance. Some would fit all of the above characteristics.

I suspected some of the children would arrive at my doors without something that every person reading this has: a name. I considered myself mentally prepared for the task I had been called to complete. Despite my assumed preparation, I was not prepared to fully grasp the meaning of 'the least of these.' I did not comprehend that I would care for children that had received rejection from every human being with whom they had come in contact.

Zachary truly encapsulated the concept of being the least of these. Zachary was a very small boy who had been found in a park under a tree all alone by the Ecuadorian Red Cross. No one was beside him or anywhere near him. He was severely disabled both physically and mentally. He could not sit, kneel, stand, crawl, or walk. He was unable to move his limbs, his torso or his head. He did not speak or communicate. He appeared to be approximately two years old. Zachary was small, disabled, and alone, possibly left to die. He was taken to the Red Cross shelter where he was kept for almost a week.

When no family member came to claim him, orphanages started getting calls to receive this child. One after another, each orphanage refused to open their doors to this extremely needy child. His disabilities, his size, his physical condition were all factors in their refusal to aid the child who needed them so desperately.

Precious Miracles had been opened a mere two months when Zachary was found, so we were not really on the map yet. Because of my prior efforts in contacting other orphanages, a few people were aware of our existence. When the psychologist at the Red Cross called her fifth orphanage, the head nun said, "Precious Miracles is just opening up, I'm sure Stacey will take anyone!"

When I received the phone call, I heard the voice on the line say, "Please, take this little boy. We have called everyone we know, but each of them is refusing."

Those words made my heart ache. But they were also the ones that I needed to hear. I closed my eyes and quietly prayed, "Lord, this little one truly is considered the least of these, and you have called me to care for the ones no one else will. Give me peace if it is your will that I meet this child."

I smiled as I felt a rush of emotion come over me. I was with my friend Jessica at the time, and I ran to her and said in true crime-fighting, super-hero fashion, "Let's go, there's a precious miracle who needs us!"

We took a cab down to the Red Cross facility and met the little boy who had no identity, birth date, and essentially no place in this world. As the psychologist began to prepare the documents for his transfer to my home, she asked me, "What shall we call him?"

"His name is Zachary," I replied. "I'm naming him after my brother."

Zachary has been part of the Precious Miracles foundation for over six years. He is the veteran miracle. His mental and physical impairments have not been erased. He still is unable to do much of what he was unable to do when I first became his mommy. In spite of his disabilities, Zachary has taught me so much. When his basic needs are met, he is truly content and completely peaceful.

Flor's arrival to our home paralleled Zachary's. She too was rejected by the world that surrounded her. She was physically and mentally impaired and had been abandoned by her family. She was also unable to move her body, communicate her needs, or be fed easily. She had been rejected by several institutions before we were aware of her existence. Upon receiving her into our home, I went through her medical file. I was stunned at what I saw in big red letters: 'Child has been diagnosed with HIV." I dropped the folder on my desk and cried. I had not been told of Flor's diagnosis, and I was taken aback by the thought.

I quickly called the orphanage that had sent her to me. "A child having HIV is a big deal!" I exclaimed. "It was terribly unethical of you not to mention that fact."

"We knew you were the only place who would take a child that has as many disabilities as she does," they said. "And we were pretty sure even you might not take her if you knew that detail."

"So you lied to me?" I asked.

"We had no choice."

I hung up the phone in despair and took a slow deep breath. As I sat there in my office, I was reminded of God's sovereignty. Nothing gets past Him. He either ordered this or permitted this. "Lord you know why they kept this information from me. I trust that this little girl is supposed to be in my home. I trust that you have a plan for her life." And right then and there, I promised myself to do everything possible to give her a happy life, regardless of its certain brevity.

We had Flor tested three more times for HIV and each one of our tests came back negative. She did not have HIV. I knew in my heart that God had allowed her first test to show up positive so that she would be refused entry to the other institutions. She was meant to be a precious miracle, and He used a faulty test to allow that to happen.

Flor is a remarkable child. Like Zachary, her physical state has not improved immensely. She remains a child with severe disabilities. But she also remains sweet, gentle and content with her life. She does not require very much to be happy. She requires a full tummy, dry clothes, a comfortable place to sit or lie, and someone to hold her and swap smiles with her.

Zachary and Flor continue to be very handicapped children. But in some ways I think we are the ones with the handicap. We worry, fret and lose sleep over things that are meaningless to them. They are so innocent and untainted by this world. Their lives are simple in spite of the complications of their health and the functions they are unable to perform. Their relationships with the people around them are unassuming, uncomplicated, unconditional and undemanding.

They are both a constant living reminder that this world is not where we belong. They truly are in the world but not of it. Seeing their lives on this earth makes me long for heaven. I impatiently wait for the day when we are in the direct presence of our Father.

On that day, I believe we will all become more like Zachary and Flor. We will live purely like they do now. We will discard the problems, doubts, and fears of this world. We will love others as genuinely as they do. We will know absolute joy and peace as they do. How wonderful and amazing it will be when we will be healed of our handicaps and become more like these two precious miracles.

4

liliana
A Miraculous Transformation

A frequent question that I get asked when I am speaking at churches or conferences about Precious Miracles is: "Where do all the children come from?" While I was still in the setting-up phase of the foundation and was awaiting government approval, I went several places to put the word out about our existence. I visited the children's hospital, the maternity hospital, and even the local police stations. I was also invited to join in an organization designed for Orphanage Directors. We would meet monthly and discuss anything from legal issues, to a child's difficult behavior, to staffing needs. Because most of the orphanages in Ecuador are run by the Roman Catholic Church, many times I was the only one in the meetings not wearing a nun's habit.

When the Foundation did receive its approval status, I contacted the hospitals, orphanages and police to make them aware that I was able to take in children. Almost every child that came to our home began with a phone call. After praying and then determining if we were able to take in the child, I would drive to the necessary location to receive him or her.

Liliana's arrival to my family did not follow the typical

procedure. With my nutrition books open all over my desk, I had been planning the next month's menu when I received the desperate phone call from a social worker of a prominent adoption agency in Quito. As quickly as April could get the words out of her mouth, she told me Liliana's story. Liliana had been left by her prostitute mother at a day care three days earlier. Her mother had not been back to retrieve her, and the day care director had taken Liliana home both nights to stay with her. It was assumed that Liliana had been abandoned and that her mother would not return for her. The day care director, despite being very kindhearted, could not keep Liliana and had contacted the adoption agency. April had called a few other institutions, but because of the high probability that Liliana could have HIV, she had been turned down again and again. April frantically asked me if I had room for Liliana. I took a deep breath and said that I could take her.

I called my mom and asked if she could come over as soon as possible. She giddily said that she was on her way. Then I bowed my head at my desk and said, "Lord, I didn't really have time to pray and ask you about this one. I think that the urgency in April's voice was enough for me to realize that this little girl is supposed to be in my home. Please guide me as I care for this child."

I raced around the house trying to organize it for an addition to my family. "Usually mothers get nine months to prepare for this!" I muttered under my breath. I had just finished putting clean sheets on an unoccupied crib when the door bell rang. April came into my house holding little Liliana in her arms. Liliana looked around with the widest eyes I had ever seen. She seemed completely petrified. Her very kinky curly hair was sticking out of her scalp in every possible direction. She clung on to April, and I approached them. Liliana jumped into my outstretched arms maintaining her wide-eyed look. She was taking in all the sights and sounds that surrounded her. The other children looked up at her excitedly, but her expression did not change. I held her in my arms, and she gripped me so tightly she was pinching the skin under my clothes.

We went to the office to complete the formalities of her entry into our home. I was unable to release her grasp on me and put her down, so I signed papers with her still clutching me. When we had finished, April thanked me profusely and was out the door in a flash. I turned to my mom asking her to join me upstairs as we set out to clean her up.

We were very routinely going to give Liliana her first bath as we did with every child upon their arrival. I set out a fluffy pink towel and a cute little dress to put her in afterwards. Then I proceeded to undress her. As I removed her clothing, I gasped.

Liliana had a two inch-long growth protruding from her bellybutton. I learned later that it was a hernia, and it was a result of excessive crying and screaming. Liliana's skin was bumpy and white and was covered in what seemed like a mixture of boils and bug bites.

I looked dreadfully at my mom and said, "What is that?"

"I don't know!" she said. By this time Liliana was crying. I attempted to talk soothingly to her to calm her down but got no result. She started kicking and fighting us. I called one of the staff to come give us a hand. Between the three of us, we could hardly control this nine month old little baby. It was astounding and exhausting.

When we removed her from the water and dressed her, she calmed down. After dressing her, I told my mom I wanted to take her immediately to the pediatrician to have her looked at. So that's what we did. Dr. Castillo was happy as always to see us and very patiently began to examine Liliana.

Upon seeing her skin, he immediately diagnosed her with scabies, an infectious disease of the skin caused by a mite. Scabies mites burrow into the skin, producing pimple-like irritations. He also stated that she had head lice. He observed the hernia and said that it would require an operation. He wanted to do blood work on her to rule out HIV and other STD's, and to see how her iron and other nutrient levels were. I felt overwhelmed by the information that he was giving me. "What have I done?" I thought to myself. "Who is this child and why has God seen fit for me to care for her? She is going to require more than I can give."

I took a deep, exaggerated breath and asked Dr. Castillo to break it down for me. "Where do we start?" I asked. "Help me prioritize her needs right now."

Dr. Castillo kindly explained scabies to me. It is a terribly contagious and harmful disease. She was probably excruciatingly uncomfortable with the itchiness, burning and stinging of her skin. The first thing we needed to do was treat the scabies and head lice.

He prescribed an ointment that I was to put on her skin twice a day. I was to administer it with gloves on. He insisted that my skin, could never be in contact with this ointment because it was extremely powerful medicine. "But I can put it on a nine month old?" I asked with my voice raised.

"It's the only way, Stacey," he said, "this is the worst case of scabies I have ever seen."

After applying the medicine to her skin I was to let it soak in and dry before I dressed her. She had to be covered from her neck to her toes with clothing so as not to pass on this disgusting disease to the other children or staff. I explained to him that I had already held her in my arms (as I was doing at that very moment) and he shook his head and said, "You'll most likely get it." Her clothes, pajamas, sheets, and towels needed to be washed after every single use. I was not to wash them with any of the other children's clothes. After washing them, I was to boil them on the stove for 20 minutes. He also prescribed a very potent lice shampoo. Liliana's hair was so thick and curly, he recommended that we just shave her little head.

Liliana was to be treated with this prescription for two weeks. After two weeks, he would check to see if the scabies were gone, and then we could proceed with the blood work.

We could also begin to discuss her hernia operation.

I thanked Dr. Castillo, paid our bill, and we got back in the car and drove to the pharmacy to pick up the necessary medication before driving home. I felt weighed down with all the information I had been given. At home, I went through the closets looking for clothes that were her size and pulled out several outfits that had long sleeves and long pants. In the meantime, my mom found several sleeper pajamas that zipped all the way up. I moved her crib to a room with only two other children in it and made sure the cribs were far apart. I wrote a note in the staff log by their time clock sheets. In the note, I informed the employees that I would be solely responsible for Liliana's care including all her diapering and that under no circumstances were they to remove her clothing. I added her name to the diaper changing chart that hung in the bathroom and to the food chart that hung on the refrigerator. I pulled out several copies of our med sheets and added them to the binder that remained in the upper cabinet with all the medicines. I filled in the blanks with her medicines, dosages, and when they were to be taken.

I looked at her bouncy curls, and it tore me up to think about shaving them all off. So I decided to give the lice treatment a chance. I slathered the terribly smelling shampoo on and then covered her head with a shower cap. She was calm and made no attempt to struggle. Because of her reaction to her earlier bath, I was stunned at her acquiescence.

After washing out the lice treatment, I continued with Dr. Castillo's list of instructions. I put on gloves and spread the prescribed ointment all over her tiny frame. As I waited for it to dry, I knelt down in front of her. I looked into her eyes and said, "Oh Liliana. I am so sorry you have had such a traumatic day. I cannot even begin to imagine what you must be feeling right now. You must be overwhelmed. I will be your Mommy for awhile. God sent you to me and I love you. I'm sorry your head hurts and your skin hurts. But you will be all better soon." And then she smiled. It was the first smile I had seen come across that scarred little face. She smiled at me as if she understood every word I had just said to her. Against the doctor's orders, I pulled her close to me and rocked her back and forth.

From that day forward, I followed the doctor's guidelines religiously. Every morning I would put her ointment on her, let it dry and dress her. While she ate breakfast, I would strip her bed and take her pajamas and sheets and wash them and then boil them. On one occasion, my dad came over to visit and asked what I was cooking. I laughed as I lifted the sheet with my wooden spoon and said, "We ran out of food so I'm cooking the clothes!"

At night after her bath I would follow the same procedure with her day clothes and towel. The lice were gone by the second day and none of the other children caught them. Miraculously, no one caught scabies either. At the end of the second week, we went back to see Dr. Castillo. "She looks amazing," he said to me.

And she did. Liliana's skin was clear, and we discovered that she had the most beautiful dark complexion under all that mess. Her curls (which I had not needed to shave) were healthy and tamed back into two pony tails. She had a giant smile on her face and she was well. In the weeks that followed, we did blood tests, and to our absolute delight found that she had no disease or illness in her system. Dr. Castillo himself performed her hernia operation, and her absolute turnaround was one of the most remarkable I had ever witnessed.

Almost two years later, we were just a week away from Liliana's departure from Precious Miracles. I had met her parents and had taken their photo. With the photos we proceeded to begin the adaptation process. Every day and usually several times a day, I would take Liliana to our living room and sit her down in my lap. I would explain to her that I had been her mommy for a little while, but that now it was time for her to meet her permanent mommy and she had a permanent daddy with her. I would show her the photos of her parents and tell her their names repeatedly. I explained that one day they would come to this house and that after a few days of getting to know them, she would leave and go to her permanent house.

At first, she refused. "I don't want to go to another house," she would say. "I want to stay in this house with Mommy Stacey."

But I persisted with the story day after day, explaining that this is what happened with all the children in our home. I reminded her that her friend James had left just a few months earlier to his permanent home and now it was going to be her turn next. She began to accept the idea more and more. We reached the point where I would take her up to the living room and sit her in my lap, and she would tell me how it was going to happen. "Soon, my permanent Mommy and my permanent Daddy are going to come here and play with me and buy me toys, and then I'm going to go with them to my forever house," she would explain. "And then when I get even bigger, I will come visit you again."

I nodded, inhaled deeply and said, "Yes, that's right Sweetie. That's exactly right."

Every time a child was adopted from Precious Miracles was bittersweet for me. I was always so excited that a family was being completed when a child had her parents and a couple had their child. I had no intention of raising each child forever. The plan had always been for each child to be able to enjoy the beautiful gift of a home. Sometimes it is hard to tell your heart what your mind knows to be true. I knew that Liliana would receive far more one on one attention with her family. I knew she would soon go to school, grow into a beautiful young lady and that my work with her had been completed.

But after loving each one of my kids unconditionally as only a mother can, it felt like my own heart was being ripped out of my chest. What would my days look like and sound like without Liliana in our home?

The Sunday before she met her parents, I took her to church with me, knowing it would be my last time to do so. As we sat side by side on the church pew, the next song came up on the screen:

Blessed be your name in the land that is plentiful, where your streams of abundance flow, blessed be your name. Blessed be your name when I'm found in the desert place, though I walk through the wilderness, blessed be your name. Every blessing you pour out I'll turn back to praise. And when the darkness closes in, Lord still I will say,

Blessedbethenameofthe Lord, Blessedbeyourname. Blessed be the name of the Lord, Blessed be your glorious name.

Blessed be your name when the sun's shining down on me, when the world's all as it should be, blessed be your name. Blessed be your name on the road marked with suffering, though there's pain in the offering, blessed be your name.

Blessedbethenameofthe Lord, Blessedbeyourname. Blessed be the name of the Lord, Blessed be your glorious name.

You give and take away, You give and take away, my heart will choose to say, Lord blessed be your name.
        Written by Beth Redman & Matt Redman.

Tears were streaming down my face as I sang the words: "there's pain in the offering." "Lord," I prayed, "I know I have to release this little one to your perfect will and to your ultimate care. Please let me say, 'Blessed be your name' when that time comes. You gave her to me and now you will take her away. That has always been the plan. Please help me accept your plan and to bless your name for it."

Several days later, the arranged day for Liliana's adoptive parents to meet their daughter arrived. We had agreed on a time that afternoon for them to come to the house. They would stay just a few hours the first day and then longer the next day and so on, until I felt Liliana was ready to make the giant change to her new home. After her afternoon nap, we dressed Liliana up in a pretty dress and fixed her unruly curls. Then I took her back up to the living room for one last explanation of the days' events.

"Pretty soon your parents will come," I instructed. "Are you ready to meet them?"

She nodded and just then the doorbell rang. One of the employees went to open our big black gate that led to the street. From the second story living room window, we could see out to the front door. Liliana ran to the window and pulled it open. Then poking her head out she shouted, "Hi Mom and Dad, I'm Liliana!"

Liliana's adaptation went smoothly, and within four days we were throwing her a big happy goodbye party and she was gone. After two months in her new home, I went to visit Liliana and her family to see how they were doing and how the adjustment had been. When I arrived, Liliana threw her arms around me and I was taken back in my memory to the day I met her and those same arms had squeezed my neck.

"Look how far she has come," I mused to myself.

After visiting awhile and discovering that everything was going smoothly and comfortably, Liliana's mother said something I'll never forget.

"You know," she began, "We believe in God, but we never

prayed before Liliana arrived."

But from the first day she came, she outright refused to eat a meal if we did not first thank God for it. Liliana taught us that everything we have is a gift from God and now we pray and thank Him for our food, our home, and most importantly for our new daughter."

I felt tears surfacing as I listened to her words. Liliana had just celebrated her third birthday, and she was already a light in a darkened world. She was a light in her parents' darkened home. I smiled as I clearly saw an open door to witness to this family.

I shared with them the plan of salvation and gave them directions to a nearby church that was a daughter church to the one my parents had planted many years ago.

Not a day goes by that I don't feel totally blessed to have been a part of each of the Precious Miracles' stories. Each child has marked me so permanently and I can say with all sureness today,

Every blessing you pour out I'll turn back to praise. When the darkness closes in, Lord still I will say, Blessed be the name of the Lord, Blessed be your name. Blessed be the name of the Lord, Blessed be your glorious name.

5

Carlos
Medically Inexplicable

I knew some of the children that would come to the Precious Miracles home would come without a name. I had made the decision to name these children after my relatives. Starting with my immediate family, continuing with my grandparents, and then on down the list of my extended family, the children would receive their names. It was enjoyable for me to give a child who lacked everything in life, a name with significance. On the other hand, I was giving all my relatives namesakes.

It was early on in the existence of our foundation, and I had named only two children; one after my father and one after my brother. My paternal grandfather had the same name as my father, so his name had already been used. The next male name on my list was Carl, for my maternal grandfather.

One morning, I received a phone call asking about the possibility of admitting a little boy. The social worker on the phone was being thoroughly honest in explaining his condition. She clearly stated that this child had severe handicaps, both mentally and physically. My heart sank as I considered the difficulty of taking in a child as needy as she was describing. She continued down her list of characteristics, and I cut her off abruptly.

"What's his name?" I asked.

41

"Um let's see," she said, and I heard the shuffling of papers. "Carlos—His name is Carlos."

"When and where should I pick him up?" was my next question.

She sounded a bit shocked as she asked, "How did you make that decision so quickly?"

"It's his name," I said. "The next little boy at Precious Miracles was going to be Carlos, so this must be him."

I made arrangements to meet Carlos along with both of his biological parents at a neurologist's office the next day. The idea behind this meeting was to have him examined by the doctor so I would know up front exactly what kind of treatment and care he needed.

The following afternoon I drove to the medical center. As I walked in the main entrance, I saw a petite, young woman in a green track suit with a small child bundled up in her arms. Next to her stood a tall, thin, man with pronounced wrinkles across his forehead. I introduced myself and shook both of their hands. I turned to the woman and began to inquire about her son. When I started talking to her, the man stopped me.

"She's deaf and mute," he explained.

"And you are Carlos' father?" I asked.

He answered affirmatively. He went on to give me the details of his situation. He had a family of his own with another woman, and he was unable to care for Carlos or Carlos' mother. She, in turn, was having an extremely difficult time working with her hearing impairment along with her very sick little boy. She was an orphan herself and had no relatives to help her. She cried as she handed me her son to hold for a minute. Then with sign language and the help of Carlos' father, she said to me, "He is starving. I'm starving him! I cannot make money and care for him at the same time. I must give him up for both of us to survive."

I looked down at Carlos and he flashed me a huge smile.

He had the sweetest, most contented and peaceful look upon his face. I knew that I had made the right decision to care for this child.

The four of us rode the elevator up to the doctor's office. Dr. Bossano ushered us in politely. After having our unique situation explained to him, the doctor ran some tests on Carlos including a CAT scan. He returned after a few minutes to the room where we were all waiting. Seeing tears in his eyes, I became alarmed. He turned to Carlos' parents and asked, "Does he cry constantly?"

They both shook their heads from side to side. The mother told us that in order to go to work, she had to leave him alone many times. She explained that on these occasions when he was left alone, he did cry. But she went on to say that as long as someone was near him, he was content.

The doctor continued, "He should be in constant, unbearable pain and considerably irritable." Then he turned to me and said, "Stacey, I need you to know something before you take this child to your home. He doesn't have a brain." The room seemed to echo as we all sat motionless. "I am looking over and over his tests, and there is no scientific or medical explanation for this child to be alive," he continued. "He does not have enough gray matter in his brain to keep him alive. I don't know what is telling his lungs to breathe or his heart to pump." As if on cue, Carlos turned to the doctor and smiled.

The doctor wiped a tear off his cheek. "I indeed can't explain how he knows to smile.

This child truly is a miracle. He may not have long to live. By all scientific reasoning, he should not have been born alive. He may die tomorrow."

I had already made the decision to take little Carlos into my home, and none of the words that were coming out of the Doctor's mouth were going to change my mind. I smiled and nodded. Then I said, "OK Doctor. Thank you. As of this moment, this is my child. He is coming home with me. If he dies tomorrow, I want to know that he had one good day full of happiness. As long as God gives him breath in his little lungs and a beat in his little heart, he will be loved and he will be happy."

With that, we let Carlos' mother and father say their good-byes. As they kissed their son, I assured them that their visits were always welcome and that they could see him whenever they chose to do so. I strapped him into a car seat and drove home.

My first hours as Carlos' new mother were, to say the least, overwhelming. I did not know how to care for a child that was as delicate and ill as he was. He had lice in his fine sparse hair, and his little body was covered in flea bites. When I stripped him of his clothes to bathe him, I gasped loudly. His flesh seemed to be stretched loosely over his thin bones. Having never seen a starving child that closely before, and I was shocked and devastated. Carlos was 2 ½ years old when he arrived, and he weighed 14 pounds. His little body was in the fetal position, and his muscles and joints were stiff. He was extremely spastic. It was nearly impossible to stretch out his limbs to bathe and dress him. At my first attempt to feed him, I quickly discovered that he was unable to chew food. I had him sitting in a high chair, and he flopped over to the side. I could see that he was also unable to sit without assistance.

I put some beef stew in a blender and tried giving it to him. I watched in desperation as the spoonful of stew came pouring out the side of his mouth. I filled a baby bottle up with milk and tried to feed him that way. He bit down hard on the bottle nipple, and the milk also flowed out the sides of his mouth. I felt my heart rate quicken, and the tears that had been threatening to fall, finally did. "What am I supposed to do?" I cried. "How do I feed you?" I felt panicky and shaky. Little Carlos seemed to pick up on my uneasiness, and he too started to cry.

"It's all right," I said, taking a deep breath and trying to control myself. "We'll figure this out. You've got to eat!"

I cradled Carlos in my left arm with his head tilted back. I put a few drops of stew onto the spoon and placed the spoon as far back into his little mouth as I could without gagging him. He lapped it up, his little tongue begging for more. "Okay," I said, we're getting there!" We continued. As long as I could get the soup behind his tongue, he didn't push it back out. And if he did, I scooped it off his face and kept trying. It took me over an hour to feed him that first bowl of food. I felt frustrated as I realized it was no more than a cup and a half of nourishment. But we had crossed our first bridge together. I'm not sure which one of us was more worn out.

Carlos had been accustomed to sleeping in a bed with his mother, and his first experience alone in a crib was not pleasant. I decided to try to fight my battles one at a time, and I held him in my arms and rocked him for the greater part of his first night at Precious Miracles. We had gotten a handle on feeding. Sleeping in a crib could wait for another night.

By the end of Carlos' first week with us, we had figured out how to appropriately feed him, and he was sleeping alone in his crib. We were blessed to not have many children under our care at the time, and one employee would dedicate the greater part of an hour three times a day to his meals.

Six years later, Carlos is still with us. He has hardly grown in all these years, but he is a healthy little boy. His flexibility has improved incredibly. He has learned to sit up unassisted and to move his head in response to voices and other noises. Carlos has never learned to crawl, walk or speak. His smile, however, has remained a constant. He is a pleasant, happy child.

In John 9:2-3, the disciples are with Jesus as they approach a blind man. The disciples ask Jesus, "Rabbi, who sinned, this man or his parents, that he was born blind?"

Jesus answered, "Neither this man nor his parents sinned, but that the works of God should be revealed in him…" Many people have wondered and I have asked myself from time to time, why has God allowed Carlos to live? When medicine and science say that he should not be with us today, why is he? The only response I have to this is Jesus' answer about the blind man mentioned in John 9. I believe with my whole heart that the works of God are being revealed through Carlos. This beloved boy touches people's hearts and lives on a regular basis. Is it really for us to ask why God has allowed him life? Should we not simply accept that God is sovereign, and He has ordained every day in Carlos' life? Can we just be extremely grateful that we have received the incomparable blessing of knowing this special little boy? Carlos is without question precious in God's eyes and he is undoubtedly a miracle.

6

jacque
Defying Death

"Miss Stacey, Miss Stacey!" I jolted out of bed as the panic-stricken voice came across the intercom. "Miss Stacey, its Jacque!" I ran into the house to find my employee screaming into the intercom in the kitchen. "Oh Miss Stacey, she's blue! She isn't breathing!"

I flew up the stairs to the children's room where the other caregiver had tiny little Jacque in her arms. I grabbed the baby from her and laid her on the brown carpet.

Astonishingly, the steps for rescue breathing I had learned three years earlier came to me as I listened and felt for breathing. There was no air coming from her miniature face.

I covered her little nose and mouth with my lips and breathed into her fragile body. Her little chest rose with my air.

"Dear God! Please! Please don't take Jacque from me!" I cried. I breathed into her mouth again and waited for a response. She coughed. At that moment the sound of that raspy cough was the most beautiful sound in the world.

I hugged her little frame close to mine and quickly drove to the nearby clinic. The lights were out and the doors were locked. I looked up frustrated at the sign that said 'OPEN 24 HOURS.' It was clearly not open. I fished my cell phone out of my purse and called my dad who lived just 10 minutes away. I looked at my watch as I heard the ringing. It was 4:00 a.m.

"Hello?" said my dad groggily.

"Oh Daddy, it's me! I'm so sorry about the time! Jacque stopped breathing. She's breathing now but she looks terrible. I'm at the clinic and no one seems to be here.

What do I do?!?!"

"I'm on my way!" and then a click was all I heard.

I had my eight month-old Jacque bundled in a blanket. I paced around the clinic's parking lot crying out to my Heavenly Father. "Please Lord; you spared her life this very night. Please continue to protect her." I kissed the top of her head, and my tears sprinkled her blanket. "I love you so much, Jacque. Please be strong tonight!" I looked up and saw the headlights from my dad's car.

"Get in," he hollered. I scrambled into the backseat holding my precious baby, and he said, "We're going to Vozandes!"

Hospital Vozandes was about 20 minutes away, but it was a guarantee that it would be open, and they had an ER. The 20 minutes flew by. I watched Jacque's chest intently to make sure it was still rising and falling with breath. When we arrived, I quickly explained the situation to the nurse who received us. They tested her oxygen saturation level and it was alarmingly low. They put the tiny tubes that were connected to an oxygen tank into her nose, but she defiantly yanked them out.

I knelt on the hospital floor, looked into her face, and said, "Baby, you need this. Please don't fight." But as many times as they put the tubes in, she pulled them right back out.

"We have no other option than to restrain her," said the doctor.

I did not argue. I could see that it was necessary. So they tied her little arms to the sides of the cot with bed sheets. She fought and squirmed. She cried.

"She mustn't cry, that will only complicate her breathing," the doctor said as he looked at me expectantly.

"What am I supposed to do?" I thought to myself. "You just tied my baby down. She doesn't want tubes in her nose! And now I'm supposed to magically stop her from crying?" I bent down to the cot's level and started stroking her forehead. Then I started singing to her. I told her to be brave and strong and that this would all be over soon.

She stopped. She looked over at me and then closed her eyes, and she was asleep. As soon as she did so, I realized how exhausted I was. I asked for a chair to sit beside her.

The doctors came back to inform me that Jacque would have to be hospitalized. I asked them to bring my dad in, and they told both of us that her condition was not favorable.

She was not able to supply her body with the oxygen it required. She would need to be connected to the oxygen tank and an IV for at least 24 hours.

How could I continue to fulfill all my duties at Precious Miracles and simultaneously sit with my baby in a hospital 20 minutes away? It was impossible. We asked about the option of her being hospitalized in the clinic by our house. The doctor said there would be no problem with that arrangement.

As he left, I continued to think through my dilemma. Being at the clinic would bring Jacque closer to Precious Miracles, but I still didn't know how I could sit with her and attend to the other children. My mind was doing gymnastics. How could I make this work? I would have to find people to sit with her occasionally so that I could leave and go to the house. I had my missionary prayer letter to finish, and we needed groceries. A new employee was starting work with us the very next day. I had praise team practice at church tomorrow night.

Trying to feel confident, I reached down into the hospital bed to pick her up. By now it was daylight outside, and we would just go straight to the clinic. "Stop!" said the doctor.

"She can't just go in a regular car. We will have to transport her by ambulance. I'm not sure you understand the severity of your child's condition!"

An ambulance fully equipped with oxygen was the only way to take Jacque to the clinic.

I agreed, paid the bill and got into the back of the ambulance with my tiny bundle. She was still connected to the oxygen and an IV solution. My dad followed us in the car.

Upon arriving at the clinic, we were assigned to a room with a twin bed. I asked if they had any cribs or cradles that we could use. They said they did not. I carefully laid Jacque on the bed and went to lift the rails on both sides. The bed had no rails.

"What's going to prevent her from rolling off?" I asked the nurse.

"I guess you are," she said, walking out of the room.

My dad offered to bring some things from the house. I sighed with relief at the thought and made a quick list. He drove over to the house and informed the staff that Jacque and I were at the clinic and to carry on their duties as usual. It was the first time they had ever been alone with the children. He then brought back a portable playpen, some bottles, formula, and a few toys to break the monotony of the hospital room. He was also thoughtful to throw in some extra clothes and a magazine for me.

I set up the playpen and put Jacque with all her tubes in it. Then I stretched out on the bed. I fell asleep immediately. I woke up when the door flung open. "Time to take her vitals," said the nurse.

I lifted her out of the playpen and held her while the nurse took her temperature and blood pressure. She then did a breathing treatment on her. That was not uncommon for Jacque. We had plenty of experience doing breathing treatments on her. Jacque had a condition called laryngotracheomalacia. Her trachea had not formed correctly and she had trouble eating and breathing as a result. Jacque would vomit approximately eight times a week. It was extremely difficult to feed her and make sure the food stayed in her tiny stomach. Her breathing was always raspy, almost like a snore even when she was awake. She coughed constantly. We had done breathing treatments on her since she had arrived at our home at only three months old.

I remembered the day she came. She was the size of a newborn and severely malnourished. She was on eleven medications and required round-the-clock care. She had given us plenty of scares in the past. I had brought her to the ER three times because of her severe vomiting. This, however, was the first time she had completely stopped breathing, and it was the first time I had to hospitalize her. "She can eat now," said the nurse interrupting my thoughts.

"Oh, OK." I responded. "Could you please bring me some purified water to make her bottle?"

"Why don't you just nurse her?"

I smiled. "She's not really mine," I explained. "She doesn't have a mother so I take care of her."

"Oh!" said the alarmed nurse. "I didn't know people really did that."

"What?" I asked. "Give up their babies?"

"No, take care of other people's children. The way you look at her and talk to her, you seem like her mother."

"Well, for now I am," I said smiling.

I fed Jacque her first bottle in almost 24 hours, and I continued to smile at the nurse's words. "You think I'm your Mommy, don't you?" I said to the relaxed and serene face below me. As I continued to look down into her eyes, tears came to mine. This sweet child in my arms had been thrown away by her biological mother. Jacque had been found in a pile of trash on the banks of a river. When she was discovered, she was taken to a hospital where she had stayed for three months. She was so sick and undernourished the doctors had no hope for her recovery. Now here she was five months later, still struggling to survive but fighting as hard as ever. I laid Jacque back in her playpen and thanked God for protecting this precious miracle at birth and for the last eight months.

A dear friend of mine came the next day to relieve me. She stayed with Jacque all day while I went to the house to check on the other children, return phone calls, type, revise, and mail out my prayer letter. The new employee arrived two hours early for her shift as instructed in her interview three days earlier. I concisely went through the typical orientation process with her and had her fill out her contract and other forms. Fatigued from my day's accomplishments, I returned to the hospital to spend the night at Jacque's side. Neither of us got much rest as they came in periodically to check on her and do more breathing treatments.

After four days, it was time to go home, and I was relieved. I went to the front desk with a healthy and alert little girl in my arms. I asked for the bill. The bill was $530.00.

Although that may sound minimal, for me at that time the fee was astronomical. I had been so consumed with Jacque and her recuperating that I hadn't even thought about what the cost would be.

"Father," I prayed silently as I looked through the itemized list of expenses. "I'm not sure where this money is going to come from. You have never left me before, and I know you will provide. Thank you for saving Jacque's life. Thank you that we get to go home now.

I pray that you will cover this cost and continue to bless our lives." I pulled out my MasterCard, handed it reluctantly to the woman behind the counter and smiled.

The house was within walking distance, so with Jacque in my arms I strolled home. I talked to her the whole way, explaining that we were going home and that she was all better. I told her not to get sick anymore and that God had made her better so she could stay with Mommy Stacey a long time. As I turned the corner onto our street, I saw a car parked in front of the gate of our house. As I got closer, I realized it was Susana, a good friend of my parents.

"Hello Susana," I said as I leaned in to greet her with the typical kiss.

"Oh Stacey, I was just going to leave this here," she said holding out an envelope. "Your staff said you weren't here."

"Yes, I'm just coming back from the clinic with this little one," I said, lifting Jacque up.

"Okay, well here you are. Have a great day." She said as she placed the envelope in my hands.

"Okay, thanks! You too!" I said, and got out my key to let myself in.

Jacque and I entered the home to the delight of the staff and other children. Everyone was so excited to see Jacque, and they crowded over her. I left her with one of the staff members and went into my office to set down my things. I had the envelope in my hands, and I started to set it down on my desk. My curiosity was sparked, however, so I decided to open it right then.

Inside the envelope was a check for $500.00. Attached was a small note that read: Stacey, we would like to start supporting Precious Miracles. Here is our first check to get started. I hope that you will find it useful.

With all our love, Nestor and Susana.

I sat down and cried. "God you are so good to me, so good to us. I had my doubts about how this hospital bill was going to be paid. You didn't even make me wait 10 minutes to find out how you would be faithful to me."

Unfortunately, that was not our last scare with Jacque. Barely two months passed and Jacque was in the ICU of another hospital. I had taken her to the doctor because she seemed extraordinarily ill. Our regular pediatrician, Dr. Castillo, had been on vacation and Jacque was seen by his replacement. I was told that she was fine and to just continue to give her breathing treatments.

When we arrived home, however, I noticed her finger nails were blue. I knew this was a sign of respiratory distress. So my dad again came to our rescue and took us to another hospital. At the second hospital the pediatrician immediately admitted her to Intensive Care. She stayed in the ICU for two days and in the hospital for five more days after that. When I was leaving the hospital the pediatrician came up to me.

"I really thought we were going to lose this child," he said. "In all my years as a doctor, I have never seen a child that sick survive."

A chill ran through my body as I took in the doctor's words. Once again Jacque had touched death and once again she had fought beyond anyone's expectations. She was making a habit of proving doctors wrong and surviving the impossible.

Jacque has long since overcome her medical problems. As she grew, so did her trachea. She was adopted shortly after her second birthday. She now lives with her mom and dad in a big city and has no problems eating or breathing. Her life is truly a miracle.

7

sebastian

Not a Baby... Not Abandoned...

I was driving home after attending a seminar on child protection laws in Ecuador, when I heard my cell phone ring. I reached over to retrieve it from the console, hoping it wasn't the staff at Precious Miracles. I made it a policy to never turn my phone off in case the staff ever had to reach me when I was gone. I looked at the screen and breathed a sigh of relief to see it wasn't them. I didn't recognize the number, but I answered anyway. It was a social worker from the children's hospital in Quito. Her voice sounded desperate.

I listened as she requested placement of a child who had suffered a terrible accident.

He had been in the hospital recovering for two months.

"We can't send him home yet, but we need his bed for other patients," she pleaded. She then mentioned that he was neither a baby or abandoned, and I began to wonder why they had called me.

"I'm sorry," I interjected. "Precious Miracles is a home for abandoned babies."

She continued to beg, and I finally agreed to drive to the hospital to hear the details and make my decision. I looked around me to see where I was and realized I was one block from the hospital. I parked and made my way to the Social

Work office to get as much information as I could.

Katherine, the social worker, seemed surprised to see that I had actually shown up at the hospital. She offered me a seat in her tiny office and scooted some files onto the floor so that we would have eye contact over her desk. She pulled out her own chair and immediately began to tell the story that had occurred approximately two months earlier. "Two little brothers were playing in the street about five blocks from their house," she explained slowly. "A 16-year old neighbor boy had asked them to pick up some garbage that was piled up near them. As they complied with the older boy's orders, he threw a can of gasoline toward them, followed by a lit match."

I interrupted her story with a loud gasp as my hand instinctively covered my mouth. "The boys were instantly engulfed in flames," she continued. "They were rushed to a nearby hospital and were refused treatment because their family was too poor. That's when they were brought here to the free children's hospital. Little Stalin, the five-year old, had third degree burns over 80% of his body. Sebastian, the older brother by 13 months, had third degree burns across his entire back and his left arm. Stalin remained in the intensive care burn unit for three weeks, but he did not survive." Katherine paused, closing her eyes and taking a deep breath. I stared at her in disbelief.

"Were they together in the burn unit?" I asked.

"Yes," she answered, knowing what I was really asking. "Sebastian and Stalin were in adjacent beds. Sebastian watched his little brother die right before his eyes."

My heart felt heavy in my chest as I heard those words. Katherine continued to give me the details. It had been nine weeks since the accident. Sebastian had been discharged from the hospital and was free to leave. In fact, the hospital needed the bed that Sebastian was occupying. Katherine explained that she had seen Sebastian's mother and siblings come to visit him, and they were always extraordinarily dirty. She could tell by their appearance they lived in extreme poverty. Her fear, as well as the fear of the doctors who had been treating Sebastian, was that he would likely get an infection amidst those surroundings. Katherine said she had heard positive things about our home for children. She wanted us to take Sebastian for one month, allowing his wounds to heal more before he returned to his mother.

I had never even considered taking in a six-year old child. I had created a home for babies complete with cribs, bottles and rattles. Where would I put such a big boy? Where would he sleep? What clothes would he wear? What would I do to occupy his time? I shook my head as I thought of all the impossibilities. Despite my uneasiness of the whole situation, I agreed to meet Sebastian.

We walked through the busy hospital. Everywhere I looked I saw lines of people. Was there a rhyme or reason to these zigzagged lines? Some women were almost bent over holding their sick children, others were hollering at their toddlers to stay near them.

Some were shouting that it was their turn as they held up slips of pastel colored paper, and others were cursing at the fees that were being asked from them. I was distracted by the chaos as we made our way to the elevators. Katherine didn't skip a beat as she shoved and wriggled her way through the crowd. I did my best to keep up with her.

Once inside the elevator I prayed quietly, "Lord, I never wanted a six-year old. And yet, here I am. Please tell me what to do. Please let me hear your unmistakable voice regarding the decision I must make."

As the elevator door opened, Katherine motioned to a tiny woman seated on the floor and said under her breath, "That's Sebastian's mother."

She couldn't have been over 4 feet tall, most of her teeth were missing and she looked indigent. Her hair was matted to her head, her clothes had dirt encrusted on them and there was instantly a recognizable odor of filth coming from her. Other relatives were there, and I politely made everyone's acquaintance.

As I was shaking everyone's hands, Sebastian walked out. He slowly shuffled his feet, one in front of the other looking down at the floor. His face wrinkled in pain with every step. I felt my soul crumble as I saw the little boy who was approaching me. He had suffered so deeply. He had lost his little brother and playmate. He had been living in a hospital for two months in excruciating pain. Every fiber of my being was telling me this was not a case that I would be able to handle.

"Hi Sebastian," I said. "Would you like to get out of this hospital and stay at my house for a little while?" I was shocked to hear the words come out of my mouth. What had I just agreed to do? How would I care for a child this old and in this much pain? What just happened here? "Yes Doctor!" said a squeaky voice interrupting my worries. He smiled big showing me that his two front teeth were missing, and I smiled back.

Sebastian's family got his few things together and the doctors patiently explained his extensive care to me. As they were writing down instructions on bathing, ointments, pain medication, physical therapy, dressing his wounds, and emergencies, I felt my heart start to pound again.

"Oh Father," I prayed silently, "This one is yours. I am positively not strong enough to care for this little boy. I need your help more than ever before."

Soon we were ready to leave. Sebastian, his mother, his cousin, and his older brother all piled in my car. I explained the seat belts to them and we drove away. When we arrived at Precious Miracles, we definitely surprised the staff. I had left early that morning on my way to a seminar. Now it was late afternoon, and I had returned with four extra people. The staff was indeed confused when I explained that Sebastian would be staying with us.

I helped Sebastian walk over to some tumbling mats that were in our play room. He sat down on them, and we propped pillows all around him. He had instantly become royalty in our house as we literally waited on him hand and foot. I asked his mother if she would like to bathe, and took her clothes to wash them. She showered as I set to arrange a room that would meet Sebastian's needs.

The babies' bedrooms were upstairs along with my bedroom and office. Downstairs was a guest room, the kitchen, living room and a large play room. Sebastian had trouble walking because his thigh had been grafted to cover the burned area of his back. I could see that he would not be able to climb the stairs to the bedrooms. The guest room had a double bed in it, and I was pretty sure he would not be able to climb up into it either. I moved the bed to the corner of the room and placed a twin-size mattress on the floor.

Among the doctor's instructions were to not put pants on Sebastian for a while because the waist of a pair of pants would be far too uncomfortable for him. So I grabbed some of my oversized t-shirts and put them in a dresser drawer in his room.

After Sebastian's mom got cleaned up it was time for her to leave her son. It was important that she and her relatives return to their home before nightfall. I sent them on their way with a bag of food. As Sebastian saw his mom and other relatives leave, he started to scream. I couldn't hold him or put my arm around him, so I just sat right next to him.

"I know you must be frightened," I said, trying to comfort him. "But we are all here to make sure you get better. Your mother will come back and visit and before you know it, you will go home with her." He had quieted down to hear my words and then looking straight at me screamed at the top of his lungs.

"It's okay with me if you cry when you miss your mom or when your back and arm hurt," I said calmly. "But screaming in this house is not allowed."

He looked at me questioningly. "Not allowed?" he repeated.

"That's right" I said, "We have a no screaming rule in this house." With that he stopped, and I never again heard a scream escape from his lips.

We filled a small wooden chair with pillows so that he could sit up comfortably and scooted the chair up to a matching table. Knowing he must be hungry, I opened the refrigerator. There was a large serving bowl of chicken noodle soup in front of me. I served some into a small bowl, heated it up and set it before him. He gobbled up his soup and thanked me. I asked if he wanted more.

His eyes grew wide and he nearly shouted in disbelief, "There's more?!?!?"

I smiled and said, "Sure!" So I heated up a second and then a third bowl of soup. I gave him a glass of milk. He drank it and I offered him more of that. He giggled and put his face in one hand. "There's more milk too?"

After his fourth bowl of soup and third glass of milk, I decided it was time for bed. I helped him into one of my T-shirts and saw his severely scarred body for the first time.

His entire back had been burned all the way up into his hair line. Part of his left ear was charred, and his left arm was splinted and bandaged away from the rest of his body. His right leg and buttocks was scarred from the skin they had removed. I blinked rapidly to stop my tears from being exposed. I gently helped him into his bed, read him a story and then prayed with him. He was asleep before I turned out the light and left his room.

The first few days were quite an adjustment for both of us. I was used to caring for infants and administering a home. Now I felt like a full-time nurse. Bathing was sheer torture for him, and we both cried every time. After his baths, I would apply massive amounts of ointment to his scars and then we would wait for it to soak into his crinkled skin. While we waited, we would talk, and I was truly getting to know the precious little boy with whom I had been entrusted. When the ointment dried, I had to re-splint his arm and reapply his bandages. The whole process took over an hour a day.

He called me "doctor," and every time I would smile and say, "I'm not a doctor. You can call me Tia Stacey."

One day while we waited for the ointment to dry, he began to tell me about the accident.

He told me how he had seen his brother with flames all around him. He told me that they lay next to each other in the hospital but that little Stalin couldn't speak because his lips were gone. Then he asked me, "When my brother gets better like me, will he come to this nice hospital?"

My heart broke as I searched for words. I stroked his face and said, "Sebastian, your brother isn't here anymore. He was much sicker than you and he went to heaven. But heaven is so much nicer than my house!"

He shook his head and said, "There's no place nicer than this place! There's always milk and more chicken than I could ever eat! There are so many toys and it smells so nice here!"

A few days later I brought Sebastian into the living room to do a little craft. I set out sheets of colored construction paper on the coffee table and explained that we were going to make a book without words. "That's alright," he said. "I can't read yet anyway!"

"The first color in our book is gold," I explained. "Gold represents heaven because in heaven even the streets are made of gold." I saw his eyes widen with amazement.

"Is that where you told me my brother Stalin is?" he asked.

"Yes," I nodded emphatically, thrilled that he was catching on so quickly. "And someday you can go there too! But the second color in our book is black," I explained. "Black represents all the sin that we have in our hearts. When we don't do what we know we're supposed to do, that's disobedience and that's a sin. When we say something that isn't true, that's a sin. When we hurt someone else, that hurts God and that is also a sin. Can you think of something that is a sin?" I asked.

"When Kyle poured gas on me and Stalin and burned us… was that a sin?" he asked naively.

I felt the tears welling up in my eyes as I said, "Yes, that was a sin. Can you think of a time when you sinned?"

"My mom told me not to drink the milk because it was for my baby sister, but I drank it anyway because it looked so good. She spanked me."

I swallowed hard as I thought of how to continue with the lesson. "Yes," I said. "It was a sin because you did not listen to your mom and because you took something that did not belong to you. Sin is not allowed in heaven," I reminded him, referring back to the gold page.

I moved on to the red page. I explained that God loved us so much that he sent His Son, Jesus, to die for us. I showed him that red represents the blood that Jesus shed on the cross. I then illustrated how accepting Jesus into our hearts was the only way we could go to heaven. I turned to the white page. "When you accept Jesus as your Savior, He cleans your black heart so that it looks white!"

"If you clean black with red it turns white?" he questioned.

I smiled as I could almost visualize the wheels in his brain turning. "In this case, yes.

When we accept that Jesus is the Son of God who died for us, He forgives our sins and allows us into heaven."

And then Sebastian asked a question that sent a chill up my spine. "What happens to the people who don't accept Jesus? Where do they go?"

"There are only two places to go when we die," I said. "There is heaven for the people who believe in Jesus Christ and there is hell for those who don't."

"What is hell, Tia?"

"Hell is a very unhappy place where there is always fire burning." As soon as the last two words came out of my mouth I bit my bottom lip.

"Fire? Do people burn in the fire?" he asked, his eyes as big as I'd ever seen them.

"Yes Sweetie, they do."

A single tear trickled down his cheek. "I never want to burn again! I want to go to heaven!"

I wrapped my arms around this precious little boy as thoughts raced through my mind.

Had I gone about this all wrong? I hadn't meant to bring up such a painful subject. I hadn't foreseen that he would ask about hell, but I couldn't lie to him! I thought back to my own day of salvation. I remembered being six years old and how my brother had also told me about hell. I too chose to believe and accept Jesus into my heart as a way out of hell. My salvation was real and I was positive of that. I have never doubted whether or not I was saved that day.

I remembered the passage in Matthew 19. Jesus made reference to the unwavering faith of children and says, "Let the little children come to Me, and do not forbid them; for of such is the kingdom of heaven."

As I led Sebastian in a prayer to accept Jesus as his personal Savior, that phrase repeated itself over and over in my head. "For of such is the kingdom of heaven."

Sebastian was ecstatic with his decision and his book. He shared his book with all the staff and explained page by page what each color meant. When he saw my mom later that day, he explained it to her as well. "I get to go to heaven to see Stalin someday!" he shouted. "Because the red makes the black white!"

Several days later, Sebastian's mother came to visit. As soon as he hugged her, he said excitedly, "Mom do you want to see Stalin again?" She looked at him with a confused expression. "Tia Stacey can show you how you can go to heaven someday instead of hell. Mom, you don't want to go to hell. There's fire there!"

I smiled and told Sebastian, "I could show your Mom, but I think you could show her too!"

"Oh okay!" he squealed.

Sebastian, his mother and I went to sit in the living room. With a little help from me, Sebastian led his mother to Jesus' feet. Of all the miracles I witnessed in Ecuador, that specific, glorious moment tops the charts!

It took Sebastian many meals with us to truly accept that he could eat his fill every time.

He had a hard time believing that we were not going to run out of food. His absolute favorite thing to eat was fried chicken. One day as he was wolfing down his food, he said, "When it's time for me to leave here, I think you can just roll me out of here like a ball because I'll be so fat!"

He told me again that at his house, if there was ever milk, it was only for the baby.

"How could a mother deny her child milk?" I thought to myself. That seemed to go directly against nature and instinct. A child needs milk. I reminded myself that I had never known poverty and that I could not judge this woman or the decisions she made.

When Sebastian had healed sufficiently to move around, I

decided he should accompany me to church. He loved Sunday School, and I made it a habit of taking him every week. He learned his Bible verses and always had a coloring picture that he would proudly display on our refrigerator.

Another regular outing for Sebastian was physical therapy. I had to take him to the children's hospital twice a week for rehabilitation of his arm. He hated it, and it became an ongoing struggle for us. Some days the therapist would place him in a hydrotherapy pool and move his arm around. He would scream as I stood back helplessly. I could see the therapy was definitely helping him, but it was almost more than I could bear to see my little boy in that much pain.

One day as we were getting ready to go to the session, I asked him if he liked ice-cream. He said he had only had it once in his life but that he did like it very much. I told him that if he could try not to scream, and if he would allow the doctor do what she needed to do, I'd buy him ice-cream afterward. That day in therapy, he bit his tongue so much I was surprised it didn't bleed. But he didn't scream, and I rewarded his bravery with a chocolate ice-cream cone before returning home. Soon this became part of the routine. Every Tuesday and Thursday after therapy we would stop off to get an ice-cream cone. I also realized that when he stopped screaming and fighting, he would finish his therapy sessions much sooner. Everyone was winning.

As an addition to the weekly physical therapy at the hospital, we also did our own form of therapy at home. The only TV in the house was upstairs in my room. Sebastian wanted to watch TV more than anything else, and I told him that if he could make it up the stairs, I'd let him watch it. The first few times he would cry and whimper as he made it halfway. He'd say, "That's far enough, Tia. Bring the TV down to me."

"No Sebastian," was my reply. "That is not an option. The TV stays where it is. You have to make your way to it."

What must have seemed like forever to him, but in reality was just a few days of trying, was finally over. He had made it up the stairs. He was so proud of himself, and I immediately turned on the TV and let him watch until dinner time.

Sebastian's leaving was one of the hardest separations of my life. For many of the other children, leaving the Precious Miracles home meant going to a much better place. They would have more one-on-one attention, more material provisions, and the love of a permanent mother and father. For Sebastian, this was not the case.

Sebastian had been a street child. He had spent his first six years in extreme poverty.

He had never been inside a school classroom. He had been very familiar with the concept of hunger. He had experienced premature independence, as his mother would leave her children without adult supervision to be able to work as a washer woman. This had been Sebastian's life prior to his arrival at Precious Miracles.

Sebastian's mother had left him in our care for seven months. The original one month we had agreed on, had long since been over. For the last five months we had heard no word from her, and I assumed she had abandoned her son. Because of her absolute lack of contact, I supposed she also had total lack of interest in her son's well-being. He was an older child and adoption would be difficult. I was thrilled when I found a beautiful Christian family who were willing to adopt Sebastian into their home. They even took him to live with them as a foster son.

But this happy ending was dismantled when Sebastian's mother appeared back on the scene, rudely demanding her son's return. I questioned where she had been for the last five months, and she snapped at me that it was none of my business. She said plainly that she was ready to have her son live with her again. I encouraged her to think of the welfare of her child. I spoke to her of the family that wished to adopt him. I explained that they could provide for him in ways that she would never be able to do. She did not react to my words. She simply said stoically, "He caused me so much pain when I delivered him, he's my son."

In seven short months Sebastian's reality had changed. He had seen the other side. He had experienced an over abundance of food and had never been hungry. He had experienced cleanliness and hygiene. He had been not only constantly supervised, but also mentally stimulated and educated by loving adults. He had been to school. He had celebrated his seventh birthday with a party and Christmas with a lit tree and presents.

Sebastian had a taste of the things we generally take for granted.

The law was far more powerful than I, and he was required to go home. I fought the ruling. I stood up in front of the judge and complained. "How can you knowingly send a child back to a life of poverty and neglect?" I demanded. "This child has suffered physical pain and hunger as a result of his family's lifestyle! Where is your conscience?"

The judge did not flinch at my raised voice and my harsh words. He simply looked up at me and answered, "You of all people, Licenciada Stacey, should know the mass amount of abandoned children we have in our country. Why would you want to make one more suffer this plight when he has a mother who loves him?"

I was speechless, and I fought back the tears as I saw him

sign the document releasing Sebastian from Precious Miracles' custody back to the custody of his mother.

The day I took him back is so clear in my mind. I had spent the previous days preparing him for this astounding change. In the process of telling him the details of his life that would be different, I was also attempting to prepare myself. I'm not sure if anything could have prepared either of us for that day. I drove him and a huge garbage bag full of his clothes, shoes, and toys to the address his mother had given me. I also took several grocery bags full of food that I thought would be helpful for the family.

I parked my car in a precarious area, and we walked down a small hill to his house.

There was a narrow entrance and his mother met us there. She led us into a courtyard.

She pointed at all the tiny doors around the courtyard explaining that each was a house.

Each room she generously called a house could not have been more than 12 feet square. In the courtyard was a small washing stone that was used for all eight tenants and their families. It was the only source of water for these people. If any bathing was to be done it would be done there.

I tried to not let my astonishment, my disappointment, my pity, and my utter disbelief show on my face. I've been told I don't hide my expressions well, so I'm sure she was aware of my feelings and impressions.

Inside her one room house was a bed piled high with dirty laundry including the baby's soiled cloth diapers. There was a two burner gas stove with the big propane tank on the floor next to it. There were no windows and just the one door. There was no refrigerator or any other appliance. There was no table and no chairs. The smell was a mixture of burned food, dirty diapers, and mold. Flies circled our heads. I noticed a banana peel on the floor next to some egg shells. I thought to myself, poverty is one thing, but filth is a different subject altogether.

I bent over and hugged Sebastian. By now the tears had surfaced and there was no holding them back. I prayed for him and his family. I prayed that God would provide for them, that he would protect them and that he would comfort them. After my prayer, I picked up my little boy and I said, "I'm so sorry. I didn't know what I was doing. I hope that one day you will be able to forgive me."

He rested his face in the crook of my neck and said, "Please Tia don't leave me here!" I wept as I held him in my arms one last time. I told him that I would pray for him. He turned to his brother and said, "And now I can pray too. I'm a Christian and God hears my prayers!"

Suddenly I realized that God had a purpose in bringing Sebastian into my life. I had been thinking I was doing him serious damage by letting him see and experience a life of wealth and then sending him back to his life of poverty. But I was sending him back with the greatest gift I could have given him. He knew his Savior, and no matter how poor he was, nobody could ever take that from him.

8

the ripple effect

"Maribel has been in an accident!" screamed Marlene, my administrative assistant, as she ran into the office. It was 15 minutes until 8:00 a.m., the start of Maribel's shift at Precious Miracles. I ran outside to the gate to find Maribel leaning against the wall, looking faint. She was covered in blood, and I couldn't determine from where it was coming.

I gasped loudly. "Marlene please stand here with her while I back out the car," I requested. Running inside, I grabbed my purse and flew to the driveway to my car. I backed up near Maribel. "Help me get her in, Marlene. And then go put on a uniform.

You will have to cover for her shift today." I drove to the nearby clinic and nearly carried Maribel to the emergency room. My favorite doctor, Patricio Cardenas was on duty and I smiled with relief. We helped Maribel up on the gurney and the questions began.

Maribel explained that the bus she had been riding in on her way to Precious Miracles had been in an accident. She did not have a cell phone or anyway to contact anyone, so she decided to come on ahead to work. Her leg had a giant gash in it, and that is what was causing the majority of the blood. Her hand was also cut and her nose was bleeding.

"You work for Stacey?" Dr. Cardenas asked her. She nodded. Then turning to me he asked, "Is this the same girl you

71

brought to me a couple years ago who I stitched up?"

"No, that was Edith". My mind trailed off to that morning when Edith had come into work with a blood soaked towel wrapped around her wrist. In a moment of rage with her boyfriend, she had punched her hand through a window. By the time she arrived at work, the towel was drenched. With an injury that severe, I was astonished she had shown up for her shift. I had rushed her to the ER where Dr. Cardenas had sewn her up.

"Is this your employee whose son was in a car accident?" he asked.

"No, that was Yester." Again my thoughts trailed back. It had been our annual Christmas party. We had just finished our gift exchange and the ladies were putting together ornaments in the kitchen when Yester's cell phone had rung. A neighbor had called, giving her the news that her son had been hit by a van. Yester was understandably distraught and hysterical. My mom, who had also been at our party, came to her rescue and drove her to the scene of the accident. Then she drove Yester and her son, Nelson to this same emergency room. Nelson had been fortunate. Having run out in the middle of a busy street, it was a miracle that he had only suffered a mild concussion. He healed quickly and there were no after effects of his accident.

"How many employees do you have?" Dr. Cardenas asked with a smile as he continued to clean up Maribel's injuries.

I could probably fill another book with stories solely about the staff of Precious Miracles.

Each and every member of our staff had troubles and pain of her own. Many times their difficulties influenced our work environment. Many times their stories overlapped with mine.

I remember the day I was devastated when I discovered that my social worker and closest friend had stolen foundation funds. I remember feeling so betrayed and wondering why it had to be her that would do that to our organization. There were several times despite my best efforts to treat the employees with respect and fairness that I felt I was being "ganged up on." One specific time during one of our monthly staff meetings, several of the women accused me of being a cruel employer. Trying to solve the issue, I asked them for examples. They were unable, or at least unwilling to come up with one. A few days later one of them screamed at me and used profanities in front of the children.

I was distraught that these women who I had spent countless hours with, interviewing, hiring, orientating, doing performance evaluations on, giving training seminars to, could be so unappreciative and hurtful to me. I had come up with fun contests and recognition certificates for employee of the month. My attempts at appreciation however seemed futile. On one occasion, an employee went as far as to call my home phone and my cell phone with threats on my life.

I had security cameras set up around the house to prevent more theft and any type of mistreatment to the children. One day, upon seeing severe bruises on one of the children, I checked the cameras and also asked the employees to tell me what had occurred. When all the evidence pointed to one of my staff members having physically abused the child, I knew that I had to fire her. The legal system in Ecuador required me to pay her four months wages in order to carry out her termination.

We shared in joyful times together as well. Miriam, Ivonne, and Cecibel, gave birth during their employment at Precious Miracles. We shared with Ruth and Maria's delight when they both became grandmothers. Ruth's youngest daughter was married, and I attended Veronica's brother's graduation.

God allowed me many witnessing opportunities and openings for prayer with the staff throughout their crises. Their sufferings provided ways for me to share God's love with them.

One morning, Marlene had arrived early for her shift visibly distraught. I put my arm around her shoulder and asked her why she had been crying. She physically hunched over as she spilled her story out to me. Her husband had impregnated a young girl, and he told Marlene he was leaving her and their two little children. We sat down and prayed for God's comfort and His provision.

I remember the evening I received the call saying that Edith's three-year old son had drowned in a creek by their house. She had no way to get to the morgue which was over an hour away from her tiny one-room apartment. I drove to her house, where I found her incredibly hysterical and surrounded by hateful, accusing neighbors. I drove her and her boyfriend, who I later discovered was a professional hit man, to the morgue.

Then several hours later, I drove them home and sat up all night praying with her and rocking her in my arms as she bawled on my shoulder. My dad thoughtfully performed the funeral service for the little boy.

Years later, I had come home one night from a date to find Ruth passed out from pain on the play room floor. Leaving the other employee on her own, my boyfriend and I drove her to the hospital. I spent several hours praying at her bedside until she regained consciousness, and her adult son arrived to take over.

One Sunday morning, I received a phone call from Nelly telling me her five-year old grandson had died. I went to his funeral that afternoon only to find out that the boy had died as a result of his own mother's extreme physical abuse.

That was not the only funeral I attended with an employee. We had been preparing for our annual board meeting when Marlene got the call at our office that her father had passed away from complications with his diabetes. She rushed home, and the next day I tried to console her and her young children.

There was the day that Maribel had arranged for Maria to cover her shift, since she had been so badly beaten by her own husband that she was unable to make it to work.

One afternoon, Doris came in late for work, and I could see she had been crying. She came into my office to apologize for her tardiness, and I asked her to sit down. As I pushed the box of tissues closer to her, I asked her what was going on. She looked down at the floor and said, "Oh I'm so late already. I need to get to work." I insisted that her coworker would be fine for another five minutes if she wished to talk to me about anything. She then proceeded to sob as she told me that the night before, her 12-year old daughter had been kidnapped by some gang members. Her daughter had managed to escape and had insisted to her mother that she had not been hurt. With my arm around Doris, I prayed that God would protect her daughter and thanked Him for the protection and safety He had already bestowed on her. Doris' daughter was not harmed again.

On another afternoon, the phone rang and the man on the other line asked to speak to Ivonne. I handed her the phone and saw her drop to her knees. She had been told that her two-year old daughter had just fallen off the second story balcony. I insisted that Ivonne return home to her daughter, but before doing so we prayed. Ivonne's daughter miraculously had only scratches on her from the fall.

One morning after an all-night shift, Cecibel had many questions for me. She wanted to know why I had opened this home for abandoned children. She asked why I prayed before each meal and why I was teaching the children to pray. I explained to Cecibel the plan of salvation, and she prayed and asked Jesus into her heart that day before returning home. Shortly afterwards, she joined a church that was started by one of the graduates of my dad's Bible Institute.

One evening, I heard Eloisa crying as she was giving one of

the babies a bath. I entered the bathroom and asked her what was wrong. She explained to me that her sister had appendicitis, but that the doctors were refusing to remove the appendix because her family had no money for the surgery. Appalled, I told her that I could loan her the money or give her an advance on her salary. I prayed with Eloisa and sent her on her way with the money she needed for her sister's surgery. Miraculously, the surgery was not too late and Eloisa's sister survived.

Alba failed to come to work one day. She did not call, and I was unable to reach her on her home phone. I filled in as a caregiver that day wondering where she was. The next day she came to apologize for missing work. As she sat in my office, I could see that she was fiercely trying to hold back her tears. I assured her that she could feel free to tell me what had occurred. She moaned as she told me that her teenage daughter had been missing all the day before. Then at night the police had found her in a ditch, and there was evidence that she had been drugged and raped. I held Alba in my arms as we prayed for her daughter.

I will never know the extent of suffering my staff endured. I was given few glimpses into their personal lives. What I do know is that God allowed some specific times for me to be able to comfort them in the only way that I knew how, through prayer.

Every Christmas I organized a party for the women. We would strategically plan it during the children's nap so that everyone could enjoy themselves. We would eat a large meal, my mom would provide a Christmas craft of some type, and we would have a gift exchange and a few games. Then I would send everyone on their way with a large basket full of food in hopes that their families would be able to enjoy a large Christmas feast.

Every employee of Precious Miracles received a gift on her birthday and also one on her anniversary of being hired. On one such occasion, I remember calling Maria into my office. I handed her the small box with a bow on it. Inside was a simple necklace and earring set. "Happy Birthday Maria," I said. "I'm so glad you work here."

She looked at me tearfully and said, "No one ever remembers my birthday. You're the only one."

One day I arranged to have volunteer help to watch the children the entire day, and we had a Precious Miracles' staff mini-retreat. We played team building games, ate a catered meal and shared our thoughts and concerns. We ended the day with two beauticians coming to fix everyone's hair and nails. It was an experience most of the ladies had never had before, and it made me happy to know that I was able to show them some appreciation.

I tend to receive all the credit for the accomplishments of Precious Miracles. I truly could not have done it without my staff, however. The support they provided me was undeniable. We definitely had our ups and downs, but throughout our seven years together we were a team. Our foundation would never have existed as long as it did had I not had the corroboration and strength of those dear ladies.

It was not only 40 children whose lives were different as a result of the Precious Miracles Foundation. The dozens of women who were employed at one time or another also experienced a life-changing journey with us.

9

sarah
A Miracle in the Making

I watched the rain splatter on the glass of Dr. Bossano's window. It was a September afternoon, and I sat pensively in the neurologist's office with 14-month-old Sarah. She rested contentedly on my lap as we waited for the results of the CAT scan we had just done. I was instinctively bouncing one leg under her, and she jiggled ever so slightly as a result.

Sarah had been in my care since she was seven months old. Both of her birth parents were drug dealers and users. They had both been arrested for drug possession and were taken to separate Quito prisons. It is not uncommon in Ecuador for a woman to take her children with her to prison when she is arrested. As a result, Sarah had been living with her mother, Gladys, in the women's prison for several months.

Since her mother's imprisonment, Sarah had been admitted three times to the children's hospital with pneumonia. At the public children's hospital in Quito, it is required that an adult stay with each child and do the basic care giving of the child. Nurses and other staff were not responsible for diapering and feeding the tiny patients. Because of Sarah's situation, there had been no one to care for her in the hospital. Her head was shaved on one side where her IV had been placed. She had only the IV to nourish her, and the diaper she wore was rancid.

The social worker at the hospital called me to take in the sick little girl. Upon hearing the details of the case I decided to go to the hospital to pick up my temporary daughter. The agreement I made with the hospital was to care for Sarah provisionally. After all, she was not an abandoned child, just one in a crisis situation. Precious Miracles would care for Sarah until Gladys was released from prison. Upon regaining her freedom, Gladys would return for her daughter and my job with Sarah would be completed.

I arrived at the hospital and sleuthed my way through the halls and up flights of stairs until I found the infant ward. I gave my name and my reason for being there, and I was told to sit on the bench in the hall. The filthy metal bench that perhaps at one point housed cushions seemed far more uncomfortable than standing, so I declined. A nurse dressed in a typical white smock with a little paper hat bobby pinned to her hair came toward me with a tiny infant. "Oh! There must be some mistake," I said. "I am here to pick up a seven month old child."

She extended her arms and said, "Yes this is Sarah. She is the child you are here to receive." I took the baby in my arms and looked down at her diminutive features. She looked more like a seven day old baby than a seven month old baby. She was so little and fragile. I reluctantly sat on the bench and laid her flat across my legs. I swayed my legs from side to side as I reviewed her medical file. Sarah had been born at just 26 weeks gestation, and she had an extensive history of hospital visits.

I knew how to be realistic. I had my suspicions that Sarah would not be a typically healthy child. She had been born very prematurely to drug addicted parents. But I tried to have faith that she would overcome her setbacks. I wanted so desperately to believe she would develop normally like other children. On that rainy September afternoon however, the hopes I had been clinging to were dashed. I sat dumbfounded in the neurologist's office.

"This little girl is a vegetable," I heard him say. The room seemed to spin around me. I grabbed onto the arm of the chair and tears stung in my eyes.

"Why?" I said my voice cracking.

"I'm sorry, Stacey. She's over a year old. She can't hold her head up. She doesn't sit up or crawl yet, and she most likely never will. She will never walk. She will never speak or understand or be able to communicate in any way. She has severe hearing difficulties, strabismus in both eyes. She has very weak muscle tone, and scarce brain development. She will most likely never show emotion. Too much damage has been done to her brain. She has severe cerebral palsy. She may never progress farther than a typical four month old."

The words echoed in the room. I held Sarah in my arms and surrendered my fight with my tears. They had won and came pouring from my eyes. "Sweet, sweet Sarah," I whispered. "Why did they do this to you?"

I paid her bill in a trance, carried her out to the car and placed her carefully in the infant car seat. I sat myself down in the driver's seat, and resting my head on the steering wheel, I cried. I don't know how long I sat there when I heard her whine softly.

"I'm sorry Sweetheart," I said. "Let's go home." I drove home that evening playing the doctor's words back in my head... "Vegetable... never walk... no emotion... never speak... cerebral palsy." I felt like this sweet baby girl had been given a death sentence.

Because of the arrangement I had made to care for Sarah temporarily, I thought it would be fair to let Gladys see her daughter. I wanted Sarah to maintain the emotional attachment with her mother so that her transition from our home would be an easy one.

I took Sarah into the women's prison of Quito to allow them some mother-daughter time.

On our first visit, the prison guards allowed me to wait in an office near the front of the prison, and they escorted Gladys out to see us. Gladys seemed very relieved to see Sarah, and she kissed her and held her tenderly. I assured her that I would continue to bring Sarah to her so that their bond would not be broken. I reminded her that when her sentence was up, she would come retrieve her daughter. I gave her our address and phone number. Gladys happily agreed. She thanked me profusely, and Sarah and I left.

One week after the original visit, I returned to the women's prison with Sarah in my arms. This visit was enormously different. I was not allowed into the office but rather was asked to stand in the regular visitors' line. I stood in that line for almost 40 minutes anxiously moving Sarah from one hip to the other. The sun was bright, and she was getting increasingly more uncomfortable from the heat. The large black gates would open periodically, and a guard would shout to the visitors allowing five to ten women or men at a time to enter. Finally, it was our turn. I was the last of our group of women, and the guard grabbed my shoulder and shoved me inside the gates. I followed the other women to another line, again waiting my turn. When I reached the head of that line, the female guard barked, "Who are you here to see?"

"Gladys Gonzalez" I said, furrowing my brow at the tone of voice being used with me.

"Gladys Gonzalez was freed this week. She is no longer an inmate."

I stood there speechless. I wondered if she was lying to me, and I tried to read her face to see if she thought this was comical. Her face remained expressionless and I asked, "Are you positive? This child is hers and I'm sure she would have contacted me had she been released."

"Don't tell me what I know and what I don't know! Don't you think I would know which prisoners are here and which ones aren't? She probably doesn't want her baby! She probably wants her baby to stay with the gringa!" The last word she said with a patronizing tone. "Now move aside, we have more visitors!"

A male guard grabbed my free arm and dragged me to the side of the office. My mind raced as I tried to figure out what I should do. I supposed I should just leave and try to figure this out at home. As I started to walk out, the female guard said, "Gladys' husband's sister is imprisoned too. She's here if you want to see her about that baby."

Quickly putting two and two together I said, "Then she would be Sarah's aunt."

"Look, we have a smart gringa on our hands," she said laughing heartily. She rolled her eyes at the male guard who also chuckled.

"May I see her then?" I asked, thinking I could possibly get some answers from Sarah's aunt.

The male guard took Sarah from my arms as the female guard searched my diaper bag.

Then she patted me down and asked me to remove my shoes. She snickered the entire time. I felt myself getting angrier by the second. She suggested I remove my jewelry, unless I wanted to be attacked once I went back to the cells. I removed my jewelry and left my cell phone on the desk in the office, thinking to myself that I possibly was never going to see those items again. Meanwhile, Sarah was also patted down and it was my turn to roll my eyes.

They handed her back to me and I was pointed in the direction of the cells. I went through two more gigantic metal gates and arrived at what they called the pavilions. I expected the women to be in cells behind bars but they were not. Everyone was walking around a long, thin outside corridor. Three large women approached me asking who they could call for me, each one louder than the next. I gave the name of Sarah's aunt.

One said, "I know her. That will be $1.00." Another woman

rubbed her body up against me and winked at me.

I had never felt so uncomfortable in all my life. Soon the aunt came and I explained who I was. I then asked her where I could find Sarah's mother. She confirmed that Gladys had been released. I asked if she had an address or phone number for her. She did not.

I told her that if she communicated at all with Gladys, to please tell her to call me. I gave her a business card in case Gladys had misplaced my number. She nodded in agreement. Then she asked if she could please hold her niece. I was happy to get a little break from my heavy load. She smiled affectionately as she looked down at Sarah.

Then looking up at me, she suddenly took off running with Sarah in her arms.

My own maternal instinct kicked in like I had never experienced before and I shrieked, "Bring me back my baby!"

She turned and said, "Stupid gringa, this is NOT your baby!"

I ran after her screaming, and I'm sure I appeared insane. She ran through a small doorway and I was stopped by a guard who said, "You can't come back here."

"That woman is stealing my baby!" I yelled incredulously.

The guard turned to Sarah, her aunt, and then back to me. "That child looks far more like her than she does you!" she said. Sarah's aunt turned around and grinned.

"What are you going to feed her?" I asked. "She's on formula. Where are you going to get her diapers and bottles?"

She was within arm's reach and she looked down at the ground pondering my questions. Suddenly, in a moment of 'mother bear impulse' I reached out and snatched Sarah from her arms. I held her like a football and ran all the way to the gate, never looking back. I reached the office where I had left my things and surprisingly retrieved my cell phone, watch and earrings.

Then I made my way to the gate that led to the street.

Sarah was crying as a result of all the chaos and more importantly a hungry tummy. The guard at the final gate looked at me and said, "Where do you think you're going?"

I said, "My visit is over now. I'm leaving. My baby is hungry."

"Why don't you feed her?" He said, "I'll watch."

The gate was slightly open, and using my diaper bag, I shoved him out of the way and squeezed myself through the prison exit. I put Sarah in her car seat and breathed a massive sigh of relief.

Less than a week later, Sarah's parents did contact me. They had completed their respective sentences and they called asking for directions to Precious Miracles. Then shortly after the call, Sarah's mother, father, and two older sisters were at our door. I discovered Sarah was the sixth child in her family. Sarah's mother delightedly scooped up her baby girl and smothered her with kisses. I took them to our small visiting area and let them have time with their child.

I was in the nearby play room entertaining the other children with a puppet show.

Making silly voices for the different characters on my hands, I waved my arms in the air creating a story. The children giggled with amusement. I looked over at our visitors just in time to see one of Sarah's sisters stuffing an Oreo cookie in Sarah's mouth. I hurdled myself over the baby gate and shouted, "No Stop!" Both of Sarah's parents looked up at me questioning my odd behavior. The children in the playroom cracked up laughing at what they assumed were a continuation of my funny performance. I gently explained to them that she was unable to chew food yet, and she would most likely choke on a cookie. They turned to each other and said nothing. Their child was over a year old at this point. It was clear to them that Sarah was not developmentally where she should be. They did not ask any questions, and therefore I did not speak in any more detail about her condition. I am certain, however; that they realized the effects of their drug use on their baby girl. They visited two more times. On the last visit Sarah had with her parents, I noticed that her mother was expecting her seventh child. I never saw or heard from Sarah's parents again. They had made the silent decision to leave her with me.

I continued to pray for Sarah that God would have His way in her life. After realizing her birth family had abandoned her, I began to pray that God would send her a family who would accept her and love her in spite of her special needs.

Sarah developed beyond the doctors' expectations. She undeniably showed emotion, and she was almost always smiling and laughing. She understood what was being said to her and communicated very basically. She learned to sit up, and then much later to crawl. She began to chew and swallow food normally. I was thrilled that she had come as far as she had.

When Sarah was about two years old, a woman named Christie called Precious Miracles one day. She had gotten my name and number from a lady who attended my dad's weekly Bible Study. She had recently arrived in Ecuador because of her husband's job and wanted to see about volunteering. I was delighted to receive volunteers, so I gave her directions and we set a date for her to visit.

Christie began coming to our home once a week to entertain the children. She was one of the few volunteers with a real sense of commitment and solidarity. When Christie said she was coming, we all knew we could count on her. When she couldn't make it, she would call to let us know. She was willing to help in every way possible. Her weekly visits soon became part of our routine and an awaited treat by the children. They quickly nicknamed her Tia Christie, and they all raced to her when she would arrive. Every week she came with a goody bag of markers and other fun items in tow.

On one of her scheduled visits, she came into my office and asked me to explain the adoption procedure. I told her the children could not be chosen specifically, but rather the adoption was done in lottery fashion. Each child that arrived at any orphanage in Ecuador had a file started at the court of minors and at child protective services. The child's face would appear in a minimum of three newspapers in anticipation of a family member claiming him. After 90 days and numerous forms, the child would be considered abandoned. Then there were court hearings, and more forms, and more red tape until the child was declared adoptable.

Meanwhile, couples who decided to adopt a child would go through their own set of countless forms and hearings. Upon completing their paperwork, they were declared apt to adopt. Once a month, tentatively, the technical unit of adoptions committee would meet. They would match up the files of parents declared apt to adopt with children declared adoptable. I reiterated that since it was all done in the committee, a couple could not choose their child, or the institution from which he came.

The only exception to this rule was the children deemed difficult to adopt. Children with special needs, children over four years old, and sibling groups fell into the difficult to adopt category. If a couple was willing to adopt a child under any of those circumstances, they were able in many cases to choose their specific child.

Christie said that she and her husband Greg had been strongly considering adoption.

With the information I had given her, they would discuss it further and she would let me know what they had decided.

Shortly after this conversation, I noticed that every Thursday when Christie would arrive, Sarah was the first one at the door, despite her mobility difficulties. She would climb up on Christie and supply her with hugs and kisses. She was always the most affectionate and the most involved with Christie's visit. I wondered to myself if Christie was noticing the child's intense interest in her. I also wondered if Christie and Greg would be willing to take a child into their home that would require so much extra attention. I prayed about the situation and gave it to God saying, "Lord. You see what I see here. I don't know what your plan is but Sarah really loves Christie, and I know Christie loves Sarah. If it be your will, please unite these two."

Not even a month had gone by when Christie asked for another appointment with me. She entered my office and her eyes glistened with tears. "Greg and I want to proceed with the adoption of Sarah," she said.

I shouted for joy. "I knew it! I just knew it!" I explained to her the steps that needed to be taken, and we ensued from there.

More than two years after Christie and Greg took Sarah home with them she was finally, legally their daughter. Their child, who had been diagnosed as a vegetable now speaks two languages, attends school with other children and is walking unassisted. She is thriving more than anyone could have foreseen. Christie and Greg have given Sarah more than Precious Miracles could ever have done. Sarah had several surgeries, including one for her eyes, one for her hips and knees. They have purchased glasses, hearing aids, and a special walker for her. Sarah went to therapy many times each week, including horse therapy, swimming, and speech therapy. Above all these things, Sarah has been loved unconditionally.

The amount of time, money and love that Christie and her husband invested prior to the adoption of Sarah was infinite. No one could have anticipated all the different therapies and medical attention this precious little girl would need. There are few people in this world that I can say I truly admire the way I do this family. To take in a child with so many difficulties, requiring so much attention and so much financial burden is truly amazing. Christie and Greg are an absolute inspiration to me. Sarah is doing remarkably well in their care. She is blessed to have found them.

When someone asked me, "Did that family choose their child?"

My answer was, "No, She most definitely chose them!"

10

michael and patrick

Triumphing Over Insurmountable Odds

Many of the children at Precious Miracles came from other orphanages. Most of the orphanages that I was acquainted with were large with sometimes hundreds of children.

There seemed to be a perpetual drastic shortage of employees and also of basic materials to provide for the essential needs of the children. Many times the children received virtually no stimulation. There were few voices, no music, and almost no verbal interaction. I visited numerous times, and I never got used to the lack of toys, texture and color in the rooms. There were no giant stuffed animals in the corner, and no baby swings playing Brahms' Lullaby. Because of the scarcity of caregivers, the children received notably little physical contact. The hygiene of the children left much to be desired. Many times they would spend their entire day in one diaper. Baths were rare.

The stench from the nursery was enough to give my gag reflex a workout. I happen to have a degree in "Child Development," but I do not think that is necessary to understand the damage that can be done to a child when he or she is neglected.

Many times when a child in an orphanage displayed symptoms of a special need, I was called to see if I could receive the child in my home. Such was the case with two very special boys; Michael and Patrick.

Michael had been found on the side of a busy road wrapped in a dirty beige blanket with a small piece of ripped notebook paper. On the paper was written the eerily lonely phrase: born September 10. He was taken to an orphanage by the individual who happened upon him. At the orphanage, Michael was placed in a small, metal crib. The white paint on the crib was peeling in most places and the bars were rusty. There was no mobile hanging over his head. There was nothing stimulating in his line of view. His bottles were frequently propped through the crib rails. These were his surroundings for the first six months of his life.

When I went to pick him up from the orphanage, I was informed that he had severe infantile cerebral palsy. He would essentially be a vegetable. He would never speak or understand speech. He would never sit, crawl, stand, or walk. I brought him into my home knowing the medical diagnosis, but also knowing that my God is not bound by medical diagnoses.

Michael is a child with special needs. He has been severely affected by the neglect he experienced in the first six months of his life. He definitely was behind in his development. But he did develop. Slowly but consistently, he began to hit milestone after milestone. He proved the doctors and their conclusions wrong by sitting, crawling, standing, walking, running, and climbing. He speaks and understands other's speech.

He was determined to get out of diapers, and he practically toilet-trained himself.

If I had to describe Michael with just one word it would be "determined." Never before or after him have I met a child that was as strong-minded and firm in his character. All children at one point like to be babied. All children like to be cuddled and taken care of when they are not well. When a child falls, he wants to be picked up and he wants to have some extra attention and tenderness. Not Michael. While he was learning to walk, he was awkward and floppy. He fell frequently. But every time without exception he would pick himself back up on his own. If someone tried to help him up, his hand would flail, and he would make an annoyed grunt. In his particular way, he would be saying, "Don't treat me like a baby! I can do this all by myself!"

Michael liked to be first at everything, and he liked to be in charge. He wanted his bath before the others, he wanted to be the first to brush his teeth, the first one at breakfast, and the first in every line. He thrived on having little helper jobs like picking up the toys, setting the tables before meals or wiping them down afterwards. One of our weekly highlights was the grocery store run. Every week I would pick one or two of the children to accompany me on our shopping trip. When we arrived back home with our loot, I would call out, "Helpers, I need helpers!" All the children would race out to the carport to help unload the back of my car. Michael was usually the first one out the door. He was able to walk, but his gait was clumsy and awkward. He would struggle to hold the grocery bag on the crook of his arm and get all the way back to the house without falling. He stumbled repeatedly. But he would pull himself up and press on until he reached his destination. Then he would rush right back out for his next bag.

Michael always had plenty of reason to play the victim card. He could have justifiably been full of self-pity. But never once did Michael feel sorry for himself or allow others to do so. Michael is an inspiration to me, and he is one of God's biggest blessings in my life.

Patrick was born in a small clinic in the town of Conocoto. Almost immediately after giving birth to him, his mother ran empty handed out of the clinic. She abandoned the son she had just delivered. Patrick was taken directly to the overcrowded, dingy orphanage. His stay there was only two months, for that is when I received the phone call. The social worker on the other end prepared me for the worst.

"He was in the birth canal for several minutes without oxygen," she explained. "Our neurologist says that he has suffered severe brain damage. He will never develop like a normal child. He will most likely not walk or speak."

I asked her to give me a few minutes and hung up the phone. I knelt down in my office. I prayed for God's wisdom in the decision that lay before me. I asked for His peace in taking this child if it was indeed His will. I wrestled back and forth with my judgment. I knew God was telling me that this child needed me. And yet the logic part of my brain was on hyper speed as I thought of all the special needs children already in my home.

Out of my eight children, five of them had severe special needs. I had tried to maintain a ratio of 1:1 of children with special needs to children that were typically developing. How could I take in another child who needed so much extra attention? A child that was deprived oxygen at birth would certainly suffer the consequences for the rest of his life.

There would unquestionably be brain damage. But God's impression on my heart was stronger than my erred common sense, and I knew that Patrick was to be part of our family.

My uncle and a friend were visiting, and I suggested they accompany me to receive my new child. I drove the 45 minutes, dodging the crazy traffic of Quito to the orphanage and patiently filled out the papers in the social worker's office. As I finished, Patrick was brought down to me. I suppose that in my mind I had already pictured my new little boy.

When they placed the infant in my arms and I pulled back the blanket to reveal his little face, I took a deep breath. In my arms was one of the most beautiful children I had ever seen.

I half-listened to the instructions on his feedings and medications as I sat mesmerized by my beautiful baby boy. I placed him in the car seat and excitedly drove him home.

As I studied Patrick that day and in the days following his arrival, I kept thinking he did not appear to have any sort of special need. I wondered if it was my biased maternal instinct that was veiling my eyes from his obvious handicaps. After several medical opinions, appointments, and tests my assumptions were confirmed. Patrick was a healthy 100% typically developing child.

Why does it still surprise me and overwhelm me when God performs a miracle? You would think I would be accustomed to His supernatural intervention by now.

I cannot explain how or why Patrick overcame his birth trauma. Neither can I understand how or why Patrick endured the neglect at the orphanage better than Michael did. But I am reminded once again that it is not essential that I understand. I believe in a sovereign God who has a plan for His children, and His plans will not be thwarted.

"For My thoughts are not your thoughts, nor are your ways My ways," says the Lord. "For as the heavens are higher than the earth, so are My ways higher than your ways, and My thoughts than your thoughts" (Isaiah 55:8-9).

What shall we say then? Is there unrighteousness with God? Certainly not! For He says to Moses, "I will have mercy on whomever I will have mercy and I will have compassion on whomever I will have compassion." So then it is not of him who wills, nor of him who runs, but of God who shows mercy... "For this very purpose I have raised you up, that I may show My power in you, and that My name may be declared in all the earth" (Romans 9:14-17).

11

mandy

A Motherless Baby

Betty was 22 years old and already expecting her fourth child. Her other pregnancies had been easy. She wondered why this one was causing her so much pain. She hoped that the squirmy little one inside her was a girl. She loved her sons deeply, and yet after three of them she was ready for a daughter. Her body bounced up and down on the red vinyl seat of the bus making her all the more aware of her discomfort.

Betty lived with her family in a remote village in the rainforest of Ecuador where medical attention was scarce. When she had gone for what seemed like the twentieth time to the local doctor, he had suggested she travel to the capital city for the last two months of her pregnancy. "I think you need to be supervised by my colleague in Quito," he had told her. "You are having too many complications."

She had discussed the matter with her husband, and he agreed to stay back with the boys. With the help of his mother, his mother-in-law, and other relatives, he was sure they would be able to manage. Betty and her entire family for many generations back had been born and raised in this community, and she was confident everyone would aid in the care of her family. The phrase 'It takes a village to raise a child' could easily have been coined there.

She closed her eyes and rested her head on the seat back, as she remembered the morning's events. She had gently but methodically patted her boys' heads. "I'll be home soon with your little sister," she had grinned as she said the words, knowing she could very well bring back another boy. "You boys behave."

Betty's husband had an uneasy feeling in his stomach as he put his sick wife on a bus to Quito. He knew the ride would be a long nine hours, and she was already so uncomfortable. He wished he could accompany her. But this is the way it would have to be. He waved at her through the window, and soon the bus was out of sight.

When Betty arrived in Quito, she was overwhelmed by the sights, sounds, and smells around her. Quito, with its brisk air, highways, excessive traffic, and millions of people was drastically different than her relatively quiet, hot and humid rainforest home. She was bluntly aware of how alone and out of place she was, and she could hardly stand from the pain she felt.

Through the help of some friendly strangers, she found her way to the public maternity hospital. She looked at the giant building and shuddered. Locating the entrance, she cautiously made her way up the stairs and in through the open door to the front desk and handed the harsh looking receptionist the paper that she had been given by her doctor in the jungle.

"How do you plan on paying for your care?" said the woman upon reading the note.

"I have a little money," Betty stated. "I thought this was the free hospital."

The woman laughed. "Nothing is free. You can stay here for free but you have to buy your own medicines, gauze, and any other materials you may need."

"My husband will come to get me when the baby is born and he will pay the rest," explained Betty.

"Hmm," the unsympathetic woman muttered rolling her eyes. And just then Betty collapsed on the floor in a pool of her own blood.

When she awoke, she was laying on a hospital cot. She looked from side to side trying to make sense of her surroundings. The room she was in was shared by five other patients. She turned to the woman in the next bed and asked, "Where am I? What happened to me? Do you know? How's my baby?"

The woman smiled compassionately and said, "They said you almost lost your baby.

Your baby is still inside you. You will probably have to stay in that bed until its safe for you to deliver. The five of us are all experiencing complications. That's why we're in this room together."

Betty's hands flew to her abdomen as if by magnetic force, and she sighed loudly as she rubbed her belly instinctively. Hours after waking, a doctor came in to the room. He routinely went from bed to bed checking on his patients. Each woman was given a few seconds of his valuable time. Upon arriving at Betty's cot he stated, "We should probably do an ultrasound to check on your baby. Do you have the money for that?"

After inquiring the amount of money to which he was referring, she shook her head. "I don't have that much."

"Well then," he said, "we won't do one. We'll hope for the best. Do you still feel your child moving?"

"Yes," said Betty. "My baby is still moving."

"That's a good sign. Just rest now. I have many other patients." And with that he was gone.

Betty stared up at the plain white ceiling above her bed as she allowed the tears to stream out of her eyes. She felt so alone. She wished for her mother's comforting hands, her husband's arms around her. She was alone and scared. Would her baby be okay? How were the boys doing without her? She had never left them before. The thoughts flooded her mind until exhaustion took over and she surrendered to sleep.

Betty stayed in that hospital bed for the next five weeks. She was not allowed to get up, even to use the bathroom. She was in an incomparable amount of pain, and she hoped for an end to this series of events. She was unable to pay for the recommended medicines and so she simply did not receive them. There was a marked class system at the maternity hospital. She was clearly discriminated against for being of indigenous descent and having little money.

After the end of the fifth week, she went to sleep and lost consciousness. As her condition worsened, the doctors began to pay more attention to her and run some tests.

Her blood pressure had risen to a dangerous level, she was anemic, and she was not breathing properly. The doctors decided to deliver her baby. The little girl was born while her mother was in a coma. The pediatricians quickly assessed the infant.

Amazingly, she was fine. Her mother's failing health had not influenced her own. She was a small baby, but seemed to be strong and healthy.

Word was sent to Betty's husband that his wife was not doing well and that his daughter had been born. Leaving his boys with their grandmothers, he arrived in Quito as soon as possible. He went to visit his wife and found her still in a coma. He ran his hand over her forehead. A nurse came in and placed his daughter into his arms. He looked into the face of his baby girl. "She looks exactly like my wife!" he stated. He asked the nurse if they could care for the baby in the hospital nursery a few more days. "Please take care of her until my wife is better," he pleaded. The nurse nodded. He turned back to his wife. "Please get better, please wake up. I can't do this without you. Your children need you. I need you."

Three days after her baby was born Betty regained consciousness. She turned her head and saw her husband sitting next to her. He grabbed her hand and said, "You're awake!"

"Where's the baby?" she asked impulsively. "Is it alright?"

Her husband smiled at her and said, "Yes. She's perfect."

"She?!" she gasped. "We have a girl?"

Again smiling, "Yes," was his reply.

Minutes later, Betty took her last breath on this earth. She had been far too sick. She had needed more treatment and better care. She had been discriminated against because of her economic status. And now she was gone, leaving three little boys and a newborn girl without a mother.

Betty's husband did not know how to react. He did not have the money to pay the hospital. And he most certainly did not have money to bury his wife. What would he do with a fourth child on his own? How would he care for an infant? And to make matters worse, she was identical to the woman he had lost. Feeling no escape from these problems, he fled the hospital. The hospital staff searched for him, but he was gone.

"What is going to become of this infant?" one nurse inquired.

"We must call the Saint Vincent de Paul orphanage" said the social worker. They called the orphanage and told them they had a newborn girl who needed placement. The baby was kept at the orphanage for almost three months. Her facial features were consistent with those of a child with Down's syndrome and upon this discovery, the social worker called Precious Miracles.

The orphanage did not have the medical staff or the economic resources to care for children with special needs. They already knew that caring for special needs children was our area of expertise! I readily agreed to take the little girl into our home. She still did not have a name, and I named her Mandy after my brother's wife who coincidentally is one of my dearest friends.

In the days that followed Mandy's arrival to our home, we had tests done to determine if she did in fact have Down's syndrome. We were also curious about her possibly having some other type of medical condition because of her premature and distressing birth.

Every one of the tests came out negative. She was a healthy, typical developed little girl.

Just three months after Mandy's arrival at Precious Miracles, I received a phone call from a missionary in Puyo. Patty Sue had established her own orphanage in the jungle city and we had met briefly once. The reason for her phone call was to ask if I had a baby girl born at the maternity hospital with the last name Tiwi. She informed me that she had three brothers with that last name, and they were trying to locate the baby sister. I recalled immediately that Tiwi was Mandy's last name.

Patty Sue explained that the boys' father had dropped them off at her orphanage temporarily. His promise was to try to get a stable job and get back on his feet. When his life was more secure, he would return for his boys. He had mentioned to her that he had a daughter in Quito but he was unaware of her whereabouts. Through Patty Sue's detective work she had found the "missing" child. We knew it was imperative that the family be reunited. The boys were older and were accustomed to the climate and way of life of the jungle. Mandy was still an infant, and the transition for her would be far simpler than the transition of the boys. So Patty Sue and I quickly discussed the logistics of the transfer. The very next day she came with a friend to take Mandy to Puyo. We said a prayer over Mandy as we sent her on to a new chapter in her life. Then Patty Sue and Mandy rode the bus to Puyo where Mandy was reunited with her brothers. As soon as the oldest brother saw her he said, "My sister looks just like my mommy. I had forgotten what she looked like. Now I have my sister and I will never forget."

12

can i call you luke?

Picture a crowded, open-air market. The kiosks overflow with vegetables and fruit. The piles of dirt covered potatoes are on the ground. The shiny tomatoes are stacked pyramid style on the tables. Plastic crates are the home of broccoli, onions and carrots.

Some vendors have pineapples, some have oranges, others corn on the cob. One vendor at the end has a table piled high with fish. The rows between the stands of produce are crammed full of people. A layer of candy wrappers, paper, banana peels, mango pits, and discarded vegetables covers the ground. The air is an eclectic mix of odors, and flies are prevalent. Now, picture a little boy walking alone through the commotion. He is so small that you would expect him to be holding on to his mother's hand. It is not natural to see a child this young unaccompanied. He darts in and out of the swarm of people. He seems lost and possibly frightened, but he does not cry. He rarely looks up. His eyes are pinned to the ground, sometimes soaring up to knee-level.

It is loud at the market. The vendors try to out-yell each other offering the best and freshest products. Buyers haggle, babies cry, nearby cars honk. The little boy goes unnoticed amidst the chaos.

As darkness begins to cover the sky, the marketplace slowly drains of people. The merchants are packing up their unsold items and personal belongings. The customers are leaving with their purchases. One vendor notices the little boy and offers him a plum. He snatches it and quickly devours the appetizing fruit. The vendor turns to his neighbor and motions to the child. Soon a small group of adults has gathered around the boy. They ask him for his name, for his mother's name, where he lives and other questions that would help them identify the seemingly misplaced child. He is completely silent, and his eyes widen with alarm. No one recognizes him. He is not the son of a vendor. No one saw where he came from or if he was with anyone.

A customer overhears the discussion and joins in. She pulls a cell phone from her purse and makes a call to the police. Feeling satisfied with her good deed, she leaves before seeing the boy rescued. An hour passes and the little boy is resting on the street curb.

He is surrounded by garbage but does not seem to notice. The last of the vendors is leaving when a van drives up. It has the Red Cross symbol on the side. A lady emerges and approaches the little boy. She asks him some questions, but gets no reply. She gently picks up the boy and buckles him in the passenger seat of the van.

The Red Cross employee takes the boy to the shelter for the night. The next morning they take his photo and have it published in the newspaper. Then they put the same photo on the morning news. After three days there is no response to the news report, so the Precious Miracles Foundation is called.

"We have a two-year old boy that appears to have been abandoned," was the phrase I heard when I answered my cell phone. I was having lunch with my dad and asked if he would care to join me in retrieving the newest miracle. He agreed, and we drove down town. Unable to find a parking spot, he dropped me off at the front door of the Red Cross building and drove around several times before joining me. I gave my ID to the armed guard at the door and rode the elevator to the top floor where the shelter was located. It was a two room apartment. There were three bunk beds, a book shelf with some dilapidated books and very dirty toys in one room, and the second room was a dingy kitchen with a plastic table and filthy plastic chairs. Sitting in one of the chairs was the little boy. He looked like a miniature man. He didn't have baby features. He was tiny, but his face looked like that of an adult. I knelt down to his level and said, "Hello!"

He stuck out his little hand and said, "Hello." I was instantly captivated. I lightly shook his outstretched hand. I asked him his name. He mumbled something. I asked him to repeat it several times but could not make out what he was saying.

I said, "Can I call you Luke? My nephew's name is Luke." He smiled at me.

Because of his three days at the Red Cross a case had already been started on him. I skimmed through the file and signed the document for his transfer to my home. While I was placing the folder in my brief case, I said to the two employees, "Please let me know as soon as his family comes looking for him. He has obviously been well cared for, and I'm certain he's not abandoned."

They both shook their heads emphatically and said, "Oh I'm sure that won't happen! He's been missing this many days, nobody wants the little rat."

I instinctively threw my hands over his ears, shot them a harsh look and said, "It's possible he has been abandoned, but it's also possible that he has a family! And I'm asking you to please contact me if you hear from them."

By this time my dad had joined us. He guided Luke and me back to the car. I asked Luke if he had eaten lunch. He looked up at me and smiled. His smile seemed to be his only form of communication, but it wasn't saying much to me. There was a bread store on the corner and I bought him a cheese sandwich. I buckled him in the car seat and handed him the sandwich. He was asleep and covered in crumbs by the time we arrived home.

I held him on my hip as I walked in the house. At the time, I had two little boys of about the same age, Jacob and Joseph. When they saw Luke they ran to us excitedly. I set him down on the ground and they both embraced him, welcoming him into our home. I went to heat up the water for a bath. When I came back after having filled the tub, one of the staff members said to me, "Miss Stacey, his hair is full of lice."

I looked around at all the children who had already hugged him and thought of how I had been carrying him in my arms. "Oops," I said with a grin. "I guess we should probably shave his head." We did and he didn't seem to mind. He reached up, felt his bald head and giggled.

After Luke's bath we had our official welcome into our home with prayer as we did with every child. We prayed that Luke would adapt to us easily, and I thanked God for His sovereignty in bringing this sweet little boy to us. I prayed for Luke's future family whoever and wherever they were.

Luke adjusted quickly and easily into our routine and our lifestyle. He had an impressive appetite and was a polite and well-behaved little boy. Because of the increasing age range of the children at Precious Miracles, I had begun my own version of preschool.

Having been a preschool teacher during my college years made it quite a bit easier. I would write up lesson plans to go with our theme of the week. I included art projects, crafts, circle-time, games and even field trips to aid in the children's development. Luke fit into this routine with exceptional ease. He was remarkably comfortable in his new surroundings.

Three weeks after Luke joined our family, an older woman and a teenage boy arrived at my front door. They asked me if I had a young boy from the Red Cross. The woman was dressed in typical indigenous clothing, and she appeared dirty and impoverished.

She hardly spoke, but maintained a steady stare toward the ground. The teenager said that he had been given our address by the Red Cross and that his baby brother had been missing for three weeks. He had brought his mother to see if they could find the little boy.

It was nap-time at Precious Miracles, and I seized the opportunity to show them inside to see Luke sleeping. Tears welled up in the woman's eyes instantly. After giving them the opportunity to see him, I escorted them to my office where we discussed our plan of action. I explained the procedure to the best of my ability. I clarified that I was not at liberty to allow any child to leave without the order from the judge of the court of minors.

I wrote down office numbers and addresses of my lawyer, the social worker and my own. I asked them to please call with any updates in the process and assured them I would be happy to inform them on their son's well-being with each phone call. With that information in hand, they left.

I watched them walk out of my office, and I sat back down at my desk. Thoughts were swarming in my head. I was suspicious that they were in fact Luke's family. Why had it taken them so long to find him? Why had the Red Cross not even given me a heads up that they were coming? How would I know with all certainty that they were his family, and what if I made a mistake? I didn't hear back from the teenager or his mother in more than two weeks, and I wondered to myself if Luke had in fact been abandoned. After all, five weeks had passed since my trip to the Red Cross to bring Luke home.

I had organized a field trip to a petting zoo to culminate our two weeks of learning about farm animals in the Precious Miracles preschool. With the help of several volunteers, we loaded the children up in three vehicles and headed off on our excursion. The children enjoyed themselves thoroughly, as they used all five of their senses to learn more about the animals. Luke's reaction to the event stood out above the rest. Luke was in two-year old paradise amidst all the furry creatures. He could hardly stand still, he was so enraptured with the animals. He would rush from pen to pen and then back again like a little wind-up toy. He had a smile plastered on his face the entire day. He giggled as we handed him a bunny to hold, he readily fed the goats their banana peels, and he laughed heartily as he rode the pony around a little circle.

The next day was Friday, and that evening all the children were contentedly eating their dinner when I heard the door-bell ring. I went out to the gate and opened it. There stood the teenage boy, the older woman and two male police officers. One of the officers handed me a piece of paper and told me that they were there to retrieve Luke, who of course had a different name. I read over the paper and told them that I would be right back. I went inside to call the foundation's lawyer, Dr. Palacios.

"Can they do this? Can they really just come here with no warning and take the child?" I was nearly screaming on the phone. I described the piece of paper to Dr. Palacios.

"I am so sorry Licenciada," he said. "But yes, in fact they can. That simple piece of paper gives them the right to take the child. It was unethical and unfair of them to not give you any notice, but they are within their legal rights."

I thought of the trauma that Luke would feel. With all the children that left in adoption we provided an adaptation period. We would discuss with the child the change of events that would take place, explaining in ways they could comprehend. I had plenty of experience with this process and usually the transitions were fairly smooth. But with Luke we were not given that privilege.

Dr. Palacios suggested that I tell the officers that our office was closed for the weekend and that first thing Monday morning they could take Luke with them. That would allow me the weekend to prepare Luke for his departure and maybe even give him a little goodbye party.

I went back out to the gate and told the officers my plan. I explained that the child had been living here for over a month and was very comfortable in our home. To interrupt his dinner and force him to leave so abruptly would be quite distressing. I asked them to give me two days to be able to explain the situation to him, to gather his things together, and allow the children and staff to say their good-byes.

By this time, my mom who had come over to help with dinner had joined me at the front gate. "What's going on Stacey?" she asked. I told her that these people wanted to take Luke that very minute. While I was speaking to my mom, the officer pulled out a pair of handcuffs and grabbed my arm.

"What are you doing?" I yelled.

"We have strict orders to arrest you if you give us any trouble," he said stoically. "We have an order to take the child and we will do so immediately. We will not give you two days. We will not give you two hours, and we will not give you two minutes. You bring that child out here immediately or you will be arrested."

"I'm just thinking of the child!" I protested. "He has lived here for over a month! How do you just plan on taking him with no warning to him or the other children?"

"Ma'am, I WILL arrest you," he said tightening his grip on my arm.

"Alright," I cried, shaking my arm violently. "I'm of no use to these children in jail. Let me go get his things."

"We'll follow you in," he said.

"You most certainly will not!" I shouted. "You can intimidate me with your threats and your handcuffs but I know my rights. And my right to privacy in my own home will not be violated. I will be out shortly with the child!"

I went inside and between sobs tried to tell Luke that his mother was outside and that it was time for him to go home. I held him close to me and told him that I loved him very much and that I wished he could stay with me forever. I told him to try to finish up his food while I gathered some of his belongings. I grabbed some plastic grocery bags and ran upstairs. I threw open the closet door and pulled several outfits off their hangers. I stuffed the clothes into a bag. I went to his crib and took the quilt off the top and folded it into the bag. I came down the stairs and snatched a toy truck off the shelf, a fuzzy white teddy bear and also his favorite toy, a plastic yellow flute. In the office, I gathered his medical file. I went back to the kitchen and opened the locked medicine cabinet. I took out a bottle of chewable vitamins and flung those into the bag as well. I told the other children to say goodbye to their brother. Then with one final hug, I took my little boy out to the front gate.

When he saw his mother, he seemed to recognize her and went willingly. I quickly went over his medical file explaining the immunizations we had given him and the vitamins he had been taking. I could hardly see through my tears as they piled in the back of the patrol car with little Luke.

My mom put her arm around me and shouted toward the officers, "This is the thanks my daughter gets? She took that boy in because his own family misplaced him! How can you say she's done wrong? She has fed and clothed and loved that little boy, and this is how you repay her? You threaten her with jail and you break her heart?"

They never looked back, and soon the patrol car was out of sight. I placed my tear stained face on my mom's shoulder. She lovingly put her arm around me as we went inside. "Let's just hope this is what's best for this child, and let's continue to believe in our sovereign God," she said. "He had a reason for Luke coming to your home, and He also has a reason for taking him now."

When we got back to the kitchen the other children looked up at me. "Mommy, why are you crying?" said Jacob. "Where did Luke go?"

"Luke went with his mommy, buddy. I'm crying because I already miss him."

"But you're his mommy. So who did he go with?" he insisted.

I knelt down next to the toddler table and said, "All of you have two mommies. I'm one mommy, and you will all have another mommy someday. Luke's someday came today, and he had to leave.

"Not me," Jacob said again. "I don't have two mommies. I just have one. I want you to be my Mommy always."

I forced a smile in spite of my tears at Jacob's tender words, and then he said, "Hey! At least he got to ride the pony!"

Suddenly something that had seemed relatively insignificant became so much more important. The field trip the day before had been part of God's perfectly timed plan. I knew I had loads of pictures of my little Luke on my camera. And in a strange way, Luke had been given somewhat of a goodbye party.

"At least he got to ride the pony!"

13

unwanted pregnancies resulting in treasures

It is difficult to know for certain how many children that arrived in our home were the products of rape. Sexual abuse and assault are not uncommon in male dominated societies, and in the more rural parts of Ecuador, they rarely have legal consequences.

The one consequence that is consistent regardless of social economic status, however, is the possibility of an unwanted pregnancy.

Renata was a young girl who had been declared mentally ill. She was being cared for on a permanent basis at the psychiatric hospital in the North of Quito. She had not been born with a mental disorder but rather had acquired her disability through trauma. I was never given the precise details on her condition. I knew only that she had been admitted to the psychiatric hospital with no hope for recovery. While there, she was raped by a male orderly and she became pregnant with his child. Although he never confessed, his crime was easily solved. She had not left her hospital room since her arrival and suddenly she was pregnant. Her mental capacities did not allow her to make a consenting decision about intercourse, and it was understood that she had been sexually assaulted.

Renata gave birth to a healthy little girl named Jenna. It was obvious there would be no way for Renata to care for her daughter and Precious Miracles was called. I agreed to take in the newborn baby girl and offered to go to the hospital to pick her up. The woman at the hospital was adamant that I not make the trip, but instead insisted they would bring the child to me. Having heard horrible stories about the way the patients are treated at that hospital, I was not surprised at her reaction. The information I had received implied serious physical abuse and neglect of the patients. I can only assume that is why it was imperative to them that I not go.

Jenna was a healthy baby, and we were happy to have her in our home. She spent only a few weeks at Precious Miracles, however. Renata's mother who lived in the jungle town of Puyo was located, and she cheerily agreed to care for her granddaughter. I visited Jenna several times in her new home where she was growing and thriving remarkably well.

Judy was raped repeatedly by her own father when she was a teenager. She became pregnant and gave birth to Richard. When Richard was still a young boy, Judy got very sick. Her father prevented her from getting the medical care she needed, claiming his religious beliefs as his excuse. Judy's condition worsened until her body could not fight anymore, and she passed away. Richard and his younger brother were orphaned.

Judy's older brother, Mark had been married for several years to Sandra. They had two boys of their own, close in age to their nephews. They made the altruistic and almost unheard of decision to adopt the two orphaned boys.

Within two days the number of children in their home had doubled. Their expenses also doubled. Their problems multiplied much more. Richard was a very insecure little boy.

He had severe learning disabilities. He was aggressive and had many behavioral issues such as stealing, cursing, and lying. His aunt and uncle never gave up on him. They were convinced that God had a plan and a purpose for bringing Richard into their home.

Judy was a childhood friend of mine, and I knew Mark as a result. Seeing their selfless attitude, I wanted to do anything I could to help. When Mark and Sandra discovered the cost of the adoption process they were astounded. They did not have the financial stability to cover the fees. Their incredible reliance on God was displayed even more, however. In spite of how much difficulty had come to their lives as a result of taking in Richard and his baby brother, and now the extreme financial burden they would face, they were still determined to adopt the two boys. Their unwavering faith inspired me.

The Precious Miracles Foundation was already assisting the family with a monthly financial gift. We had also provided ongoing family therapy with an amazing Christian psychologist. I knew in the depths of my heart that as an organization we needed to finalize the adoption procedure. Sheer joy enveloped all of us when we received the document stating that Richard and his younger brother were now Mark and Sandra's official sons.

Frank and Sylvia were also products of incest rape. They arrived at our door with their young, broken mother. She was trying to make ends meet with her two young children and was finding the task virtually impossible. She had heard of Precious Miracles and came to see if we could help her. We opened our doors, our arms, and our hearts to her small children. The effect of incest was not apparent in Sylvia. She was the younger of the two, and she seemed to be healthy and on target developmentally. Frank, however, was severely disabled. He was unable to do anything unassisted. Even breathing was a chore for him.

Their mother returned after only a few days of leaving her children with us. She sat in my office with anguish written all over her face. She looked up at me and said, "I thought I could, but I can't. I thought I would be better off without them. But I'm miserable. I can't eat and I can't sleep and I can't think straight. I would rather struggle to survive with my babies than to have to face each day without them."

I was overcome with compassion, and I sent the young family on their way piled high with gifts including a stroller, groceries, a stocked diaper bag and toys. I encouraged her to call me or come back if she ever needed anything that I could provide, but I never heard from her again.

Carolina had two other children and was unmarried when she discovered she was pregnant. All three of her children had different fathers. She insisted that the last man had physically violated her and left her with child. Carolina went to her older brother for help. Her brother told her that his wife was working at a foundation named Precious Miracles that took in abandoned and orphaned children. Carolina knew instantly that was the solution to her dilemma. She had no desire to raise the child that was only a reminder of the man who had taken advantage of her body. She came to meet with me when she was eight months pregnant and told me she would like for me to take the child that was growing inside of her. We made arrangements to admit him into our home as soon as he made his debut appearance.

When she delivered her baby boy into the world, I was at her side in the hospital.

Joshua came home with me two days later. Joshua grew and developed into one of the most intelligent little guys I have ever known. His mother visited him a few times during his stay at Precious Miracles, but she never regretted her decision. She was fully aware that she had chosen the best life for her son.

The children called their caregivers Tia, meaning "aunt" in Spanish. As Joshua grew and began speaking, he followed suit. Little did he know that one of the women he was calling aunt was truly his aunt. The day Joshua left with his family, his aunt approached me with tear-filled eyes. Almost whimpering, she thanked me profusely for giving her nephew a chance in life and for allowing her to help in his initial rearing. I reminded her that there was no way that I could have orchestrated such a beautiful plan and that God was responsible.

14

diego

A Failed Abortion

Norma had decided she was finished having children. Unfortunately for her, she was pregnant with her third. Her second child had died and five-year old Erica required too much from her. Making ends meet just to sustain Erica was proving too difficult. The two of them lived alone in a miniature, underground room in an unsafe neighborhood. The room was dark and damp and had no furniture or appliances to make it appear livable.

There was a cardboard box in one corner with their few possessions, and an old rotting mattress lay directly on the musty cement floor.

Norma worked part time cleaning a small diner. She was so discouraged by her pregnancy that her solution was to end it. One afternoon she stood with her hands on her hips in the diner's kitchen. The lunch rush was over and the place had cleared of most of its customers. She went to the back and cried out hysterically, "I don't want this child!" She grabbed the dish soap off the sink's ledge and swallowed a mouthful. "That should do it," she thought.

As Norma gulped down the soap, her boss, Alicia walked in. Norma told Alicia what she had done. "I just want to let you know that I may have to miss a couple days of work. I'll most likely miscarry my baby," she explained.

"Are you insane?!" asked Alicia. "What would possess a woman to try to kill her own baby?"

Norma said nothing and just stared blankly ahead as if she had gone to a faraway place in her mind. The days passed and Norma did not bleed as she had expected. It seemed as though her plan had not succeeded. She apparently was not going to lose the baby.

Frustrated, she tried again. The second time she drank almost an entire bottle of vinegar. The scene repeated itself as she told Alicia she would most likely need some time off.

Alicia was livid. "What is your problem?" she questioned Norma. "There are people that are not able to have children. I'm sure someone will want your baby! Why are you doing this?"

Norma again stared blankly ahead and said nothing.

A week later there was still no bleeding. Norma fastened her pants button below her growing abdomen. That day at work she became unreasonably hysterical. She cried to Alicia, "I don't want this child. I want him to die and leave me alone!" And with that she grabbed a cast iron frying pan and slammed it across her belly.

"Stop it you crazy woman!" shouted Alicia as she tore the pan from Norma's tight grip.

In the corner, witnessing the whole incident stood Maya. Maya was still in high school and had just recently started working at the diner to help out with expenses at home.

She turned to another employee and asked with alarm, "What is going on?!"

"Norma's crazy," came the reply. "She is pregnant and is doing anything possible to lose her child. This is her third attempt here at work. Who knows how many other times she has hurt herself at home. She's sick in the head!"

Maya thought quickly. "My Mom works for some Americans," she said. "Maybe they can help. They have money. Maybe they can buy the baby. Maybe they will take the baby to their country." With this thought in her mind, Maya went to Alicia and told her of her plan.

That night Maya told her mother, Rosa, of the incident at the diner. "This crazy woman is trying to kill her unborn child!" she exclaimed. "You have to ask your employers if there is something they can do." Rosa was astounded at the details of her daughter's story and readily agreed that she would talk to her employers.

The days continued to go by uneventfully. Norma waited in vain for the blood that did not come. She was not far from being full term in her pregnancy. The only thing she could do now, she mused, is have the baby and kill it after it was born. And that is exactly what she planned on doing.

Meanwhile, Rosa spoke about the situation to her boss, Amy.

As Amy listened to the alarming details, she remembered something she had just heard a week before. A close friend had mentioned to her that one of her previous students had returned to Ecuador to start an orphanage. "Let me try to find Stacey Smith," she comforted Rosa. "Maybe she can take the baby."

I answered the phone and was shocked to hear the voice of one of my former school teachers on the line. She promptly explained the circumstances and asked if I would be willing to take the child.

"Yes, of course. We would be happy to take him in," I answered, sounding more sure than I felt. The probabilities of this child being healthy and developing normally were very slim. "He may not even make it out alive. She has done too much damage." I thought to myself.

A few days later, I got a call that the baby had been born. Norma had gone to a clinic to give birth, far beyond her financial means. Little Diego was born at a healthy weight and had a high Apgar score. When I heard the news, I was hopeful, yet realistic. I was fully aware that many things can present themselves later.

Amy, my mom, and I went to meet little Diego. When we arrived, the doctors and other staff at the clinic were irate. "Who is this woman?" they prodded. "She says she has no money to pay for her bill. She says that the Americans are coming to pay for her bill."

The three of us stood in disbelief at the comments. We made an attempt to explain the situation to the hospital staff. We told them that Norma was not related to any of us, nor anyone we knew. We then asked them if we could just take the baby. We explained that this woman had attempted to abort her child and that our only interest was his well- being. We also explained that if left with his mother, he would surely die.

"That is not my problem. No way can you take only the child!" the administrator replied.

"They leave together. If she won't pay, we'll send her to jail and her baby will go with her."

My mom, Amy and I exchanged glances. I was the first to speak up. "We all know he isn't bluffing. Children are sent with their mothers to jail frequently in this country. He will without doubt send Norma with Diego to jail. What choice do we have? If we have to pay the bill, then I guess that's what we are going to do."

Amy and my mom nodded, supporting my decision, and I pulled out my check book. I had made a commitment to never, ever offer money in exchange for a child. I never wanted Precious Miracles to be accused of buying and selling children. I knew, however, this tiny little boy would not survive prison, especially with a mother who had been so blatantly adamant about ending his life. I was certain beyond a doubt that she would not care for her son. After signing the check, I handed it to the receptionist. I then handed Norma the forms relinquishing her rights to her child, and she compliantly signed them. We wrapped little Diego up in a blanket, and we headed home with our new miracle.

The employees were overjoyed when I walked in with our two-day old baby. I explained briefly his situation. "We must be on the lookout for any developmental delays." I made it clear to them that although he appeared to be healthy; he was most likely going to suffer deeply for the actions his mother took.

Shortly after his arrival to our home, I took Diego to see Dr. Castillo. As I held the newborn in my arms, I gave the grizzly details of his birth and his prenatal circumstances. Dr. Castillo assured me that there was little that we could know at such an early stage. As the boy grew, we would proceed with different tests to decipher what his special needs would be.

Four months passed and it was time to do a CT scan. The day I took him in is very clear in my memory. I had forced him to fast for four hours and had tried to keep him awake per the technician's instructions. They gave him some medicine to allow him to sleep and it worked instantly. They took my tiny little baby and placed him on a high table and wheeled him under the giant machinery. It was a surreal experience for me. There I stood in the doorway looking at my drugged baby on that table. I had such a strong impulse to run to him. My own instinct was screaming at me to snatch him off that high surface. And yet he was so drugged, it was impossible for him to wake up or even move. The test was done swiftly, and we went home to wait somewhat anxiously for the results.

When the results came back, I quickly called Dr. Castillo for an appointment. He was able to see me that very day. Nervously tapping my foot on the floor, I fidgeted with my fingers as he read over the papers. "There's no abnormal activity in the child's brain," he said. "It doesn't make any sense, after everything you've told me. But, unless something presents itself later, this child is completely healthy and has no trace of any brain damage."

"Yes!" I shouted as I jumped out of my chair. "That's amazing! Praise GOD!"

We repeated several tests during Diego's stay with us. Nothing ever did present itself.

Diego is now six years old and is a healthy little boy. His growth chart resembles every other six-year old boy's chart in his class, and he has hit every milestone appropriately. He loves school and does very well academically. He has completed his permanent family, and they are overjoyed with their miracle son.

15

sharon

Journal to a Precious Miracle

11-May-2004

Sharon,
You came into my home and into my heart this afternoon. You are five days old and your mom has chosen a different life for you than what she can provide. I'm sorry I have to separate you from your mother. But I want you to know that as long as God lends you to me and me to you, I will love you, care for you, teach you, protect you, and be your mommy. It's hard to describe how one can love someone they just met, but I do. I gave you my own mother's name. You are a beautiful baby girl, and I'm thrilled that God has put us in each other's lives. Welcome to Precious Miracles!

Mommy Stacey

28-May-04

Baby Sharon,
You are three weeks old today. You are perfectly healthy and gorgeous! When I feed you your bottles you stare into my eyes, and you have captured my heart. I feel a very special and unique bond with you that I haven't felt with the other children. I'm absolutely crazy about you! I love you,

Mommy Stacey

25-November-04

Sharon,

Today is Thanksgiving, and I wanted to write in your journal to tell you how thankful I am for you. God has a plan for your life and for your future. I have placed you in His hands and I leave it up to Him to take care of the details. Whatever He has in store for you, know that I will always pray for you. You will always be in my heart and I will always, always, love you,

Mommy Stacey

7-May-05

Happy Birthday Sharon!

I can't believe you are already a 1-year old. You took your first steps two weeks ago which broke the record here at Precious Miracles. We had a party for you today. The staff came with their kids. We decorated with balloons and streamers, both of which you tried to eat! We had lots of normally prohibited junk food including popsicles which were your personal favorite. You had so much fun! I love you so much! And I love being your Mommy!

Mommy Stacey

8-June-05

Sweet Sharon,

You have a special love and are particularly affectionate towards the children in our home that have special needs. I'm not sure how you know the difference, but you do. You can be somewhat aggressive with the healthy children, but you hug, kiss, stroke, pat, and cuddle the special needs children. It's very heartwarming to see how tender you are. And you defend them if anyone else comes near them. You are such a sweet little girl!

Mommy Stacey

30-August-05

Sharon,

You are the most fearless child I've ever known. You grab our pet bunnies even though you know they will scratch you. You climb up anywhere that allows for climbing. The other day you brought me one of our baby chicks by the neck. I was sure you had killed it, but it miraculously survived! If you fall, you pick yourself right back up without hesitation. You are very curious and you love exploring your environment. Your new favorite thing is escaping from the playroom. You think it's hilarious to go into the forbidden kitchen. You definitely keep us on our toes. You are a lot of fun, but if I have any gray hairs, I blame you! I love you so much!

Mommy Stacey

25-October-05

Sharon,

I've been thinking for some time on the possibility of adopting a child. I've come to terms with the fact that I will probably never have biological children.

Adoption seems logical. In this country, they do not allow the parent to choose a child. It's all done randomly. But I am going to do everything that is humanly possible to adopt you. You have a very special place in my heart that is indescribable. I have loved you with a different kind of love since the day you arrived in my home. And now you even physically resemble me. I would love to be your forever mommy. I love you so much!

Mommy Stacey

12-November-05

Sharon,

I've officially started the adoption paperwork for you. The lawyer says I have about an 80% chance of being assigned to you as your mother. I am leaving all this in God's hands. If He wants me to be your mom, I will be. If not, He will have a better mommy and maybe even a daddy for you! I love you princess! I hope you will be mine!

Mommy Stacey

25- December-05

Merry Christmas Sharon!

You had a fun day! Grandpa came over and read us the Christmas story, and you nodded in agreement the entire time. You really enjoyed opening all your gifts. And you were my big helper too! You passed out the gifts to your special needs "siblings" and then helped them open them. It was very sweet to watch you. I think you took more pleasure in helping them than you did with your own gifts. I love you!

Mommy Stacey

23-January-06

Sharon,

We have a new baby in the house, and you have nominated yourself his primary caregiver. You want to hold him, smother him with kisses, and feed him his bottle. You are always aware of him. You're a sweet big sister, and you're only 20 months old yourself! I love you!

Mommy Stacey

16-April-06

Happy Easter!

On Friday we made the traditional Ecuadorian soup called Fanesca. You gobbled it up! Then yesterday we painted Easter eggs. You kids are so culturally diverse here at Precious Miracles! You squeezed the eggs you were painting. They were hard-boiled, but it still made a mess. You, of course, thought it was hilarious! Today I hid all the eggs and other goodies around the backyard. Whenever you found one, you would launch it into your basket to see if you could crack it. That's so you! You had fun, and we had fun watching you!

Mommy Stacey

26- August-06

Sharon,

You are quite the performer. You love to dance around the house if we have music on. If I get the video camera out, you rush over to put on a show. When I have the still camera, you try to get in every shot. It could never occur to you that I may not want you in every shot! I have 10 other children! But you are pretty certain the world revolves around you. I love you more than I could ever express!

Mommy Stacey

5- December-06

Sharon,

We took our annual Christmas picture today. We decided to do a nativity scene with all 13 of you. I made you an angel for the sheer irony of it! You stood up on a stool next to me with your wings and halo in place. It was downright adorable. Your wings reflected your image, and in most of the shots you were looking sideways admiring yourself in them. You crack me up! Grandpa had a package of Smarties candies, and he told you all you'd get one (yes one!) if you stood still. It worked. All of you stood perfectly still. We got the shot and then you all got your very generous reward!

Mommy Stacey

10-February-07

Sharon,

I had my life turned upside down today. I have been meeting consistently with the lawyer regarding your adoption. I have also taken the obligatory classes and filed the required paperwork. Today, I was told that adopting you would be impossible for me. Because you are a healthy child you must go into the adoption lottery. Only children that are deemed difficult to adopt can be chosen. You will most certainly not be difficult to adopt. You are a physically beautiful child and you are smart, healthy, and "perfect." As a single woman, I enter the lottery at the bottom of the list. The officials at the technical unit of adoptions at the ministry of social welfare told me that when they "run out" of couples, they would consider giving a single woman a child. My argument for adopting you was that I have had you since birth, and we have already formed an undeniable bond together. They would not hear me out but, again insisted that unless there were no couples on the waiting list at all, I would not be allowed to adopt. I'm totally crushed. I feel like you were meant to be my child. I feel like we were meant to be together. I love you so much, I cannot begin to express how much this hurts me. Now I must pray that God will provide the perfect family for you. That is a hard prayer to pray. I love you! "For I know the plans I have for you," declares the Lord, "plans to prosper you and not to harm you, plans to give you hope and a future" (Jeremiah 29:11, NIV).

Mommy Stacey

4-May-07

Sharon,

I went to an adoption assignment meeting today and you were assigned to your permanent family. They would not give me any information on them, not even their names, so I have to wait for them to contact me. All I know is that you'll be leaving soon, and I'm having such a hard time wrapping my brain around that. My life will be completely different when you are not a part of it. I love you more than I can say. You must know that you are an extremely important part of my life. You are so much like a daughter to me. You're the only child after Alison that I considered adopting. We have a unique bond between us, and I'm terrified to see that broken. And now because of a piece of paper with a signature on it, you belong to someone else? I pray for your family. I pray they will have patience and that they will discipline and care for you in the way you require. I pray that they will be prepared for you. I love you!

Mommy Stacey

12-May-07

Sweet, sweet Sharon,

I got the phone call today that I've been expecting and dreading for so long. The voice on the other end said, "I'm Sharon's mom."

I almost dropped the phone! I choked back the instant tears and the urge to yell out, "No, I am!"

We agreed to meet on Friday, two days from today. I can't believe it's time to let you go.

How am I supposed to live without you? Could this person I just spoke to love you the way I have loved you? Can she possibly know how special and priceless you are? Can she and will she make you happy? We had been playing dress-up, and to take the call I had gone back to the therapy room to get away from the noise. As if you knew, you walked in to find me. You saw me crying in the corner and came over to me. You threw your little arms around my neck and held on. I squeezed you tightly and let the tears fall from my eyes. I told you that your mommy and daddy would be coming soon to meet you and that you would be leaving us to go to your new house.

You shook your head violently and said you would stay with Mommy Stacey. We've talked about this before, sweetie, and I've explained to you already that Precious Miracles is not your permanent home. But it looks like you're not quite ready to accept that fact either.

We celebrated your third birthday just last week. Precious Miracles is all you've ever known. I'm all you've ever known.

Mommy Stacey

18-May-07

Sharon,

We met your parents today. I met them first at a coffee shop and told them all about you. Then I brought them to Precious Miracles where you were anxiously awaiting them. You warmed up pretty quickly, especially when your mom let you go through her purse and try on her lipstick! We'll have a few more days of adaptation and then you'll leave with them when I think you're ready. I'm not sure I'll ever be ready. It's so hard to accept that this couple is your new family.

Mommy Stacey

23-May-07

Sharon,

Today was your departure day. You have spent several days with your parents getting to know each other, and now I think you're ready to live with them.

They are a sweet young couple, and if I have to let you go, there's no one I'd prefer to take over raising you than them. They are blessed to have you. We had a little party so all the staff and the other children could say goodbye to you. Your mom was so thoughtful and gave all the other children a present. We gave you some of your favorite toys from this house. I gave your mom a gigantic folder of all your art work, and your scrapbook. I tried to make an eloquent speech, but I pretty much just made a blubbery mess of it. We prayed over you and your new family. Then I gave you a huge hug. On May 11, 2004, I wrote that you came into my home and into my heart. Today, three years later you left my home. But my Precious Miracle, you will never leave my heart.

Mommy Stacey

Sharon,

I always knew the possibility existed that you and I were not meant to be together forever. Now God has showed us that was not His plan. But His plan is perfect, and He knows so many things that we do not. He has prepared this family for you, and I will have peace.

Mommy Stacey

A Mother's Prayer

I pray you'll be my eyes And watch her where she goes And help her to be wise Help me to let go Every mother's prayer Every child knows Lead her to a place Guide her with your grace To a place where she'll be safe I pray she finds your light And holds it in her heart As darkness falls each night Remind her where you are Every mother's prayer Every child knows Lead her to a place Guide her with your grace To a place where she'll be safe.

David Foster, Carole Bayer Sager

16

leonard

Lost and Found

It is early one evening at the Quito International Airport. Several flights are scheduled for departure in the next few hours. Passengers are methodically lining up with their boarding passes and ID in hand as they go through the seemingly endless security lines. Among the crowd, there are two tall, stylishly dressed Spanish women. They exchange words, and it is apparent that they are traveling together. One of the ladies has long, curly black hair that is gathered in a simple elastic band just below her neck.

The second lady has a short attractive hair style and is visibly older than her friend. The younger lady is holding a baby securely wrapped in a lacy pink blanket. She seems oddly uncomfortable with her bundle as she bounces her knees slightly. They reach the front of the line and approach the counter together. The short haired woman stands authoritatively in front of her companion and places the papers through the crescent- shaped hole in the bottom of the glass. The officer behind the glass takes the papers and gives the women a once over glance.

"You're traveling together?" she asks.

"Yes. We're friends, we're together," replies the older woman.

"Where are you headed this evening?"

"Madrid," answers the woman with a smile.

"And the baby's papers?" says the officer with her hand outstretched.

The younger woman quickly thrusts some folded papers under the glass. The officer skims the papers. "Awe, she's only a month old..." she says, her voice softening in a moment of maternal instinct.

As if on cue, the baby squirms in the woman's arms. The woman looks uneasy. She sways back and forth in an attempt to quiet the child. The effort is futile, and the baby wakes and lets out a loud wail. As the woman rocks nervously, the blanket falls to the ground. She gasps and scrambles to pick it up off the floor.

The older woman says calmly, "So we're free to go then?" and shoots the long-haired woman a glaring look.

"No," says the officer looking wide-eyed at the baby. "You are not free to go. That child is not one month old! Kelley, get over here!" she shouts to her colleague at the next desk.

By this time, the two women are acting extremely uncomfortable. The two officers approach them and ask to see the child. Other people in line are straining their necks to see what all the commotion is about. More security officers have also left their stations to see what is happening. The blanket is removed, and gasps are heard as a child that appears to be at least five or six months old emerges. The original officer takes the papers once again. She looks at the date on the birth certificate.

"It says here this baby girl was born last month!" she states. "What is going on here?"

Another officer chimes in, "That baby doesn't look like a girl either!" He instructs the woman to remove the child's diaper. The woman, looking dejected at the floor follows his orders. More gasps are heard as the diaper is removed and the unmistakable evidence is seen. The baby is a boy.

In a matter of minutes the National Police are called, the two women are handcuffed and taken to prison, and the baby is in the arms of a confused police detective.

On the other end of town, bath time is almost over at Precious

Miracles. As I'm zipping up Sharon's pajamas the phone rings.

"Sweetie, go get God's book, (our nickname for the Children's Bible we used for devotions), and have your brothers and sisters sit on the rug and wait for me," I instruct.

The phone rings again and I answer, "Good evening."

"Is this the Precious Miracles Foundation?" says a woman's voice on the line.

"Yes it is, and I'm the Director. Is there something I can do for you?" I ask with a twinge of annoyance as I look up at the clock. Why am I getting phone calls at 7:00 at night? Are those normal office hours to these people? "We are calling from the National Police of Ecuador. We have somewhat of an emergency," says the woman. "We have a little baby boy, and we need a place for him.

We're on our way to your house right now. Is that okay?"

"You're already on your way?" I ask surprised. Usually I am given more time to pray and make the decision to admit a child. But tonight I am not given that luxury. "How old is he?"

"About 5 or 6 months, we really don't know. He seems healthy. He's hungry and he needs a place to stay until we find out who he is."

"Okay," I say. "Of course, you may come. Do you know how to get here?" She says that she does and we hang up.

I walk out to the play room to find all my little angels sitting on the rug and Sharon holding the devotion book proudly in her lap.

"I love you guys!" I gush as I sit down. Then I say, "Tonight we are going to get a little brother! He'll be here very soon! Does that sound like fun?"

"Yay!" shout all the children jumping up and down. We read the Bible story, sing a few songs and then go around the circle taking turns praying. Just as I close with an "amen," the doorbell rings. The children run to the window to look out.

"Is that our brother?" asks Joseph.

"Yes!" I said.

I open the door and in walk three police officers in full uniform. The female officer is holding a very upset little boy. I turn to one of the employees and say, "There's a can of formula in the pantry. Please go prepare a bottle." She runs off to do so as I receive the baby into my arms. "Hi little guy," I say. "It's nice to meet you. We'll get your tummy full as soon as possible." I take him into my office and invite the officers to join me. Two of the officers follow, and the third stays out with the other children letting them try on his hat and empty gun holster.

The officers proceed to tell me the evening's sequence of events at the airport as I feed the baby a bottle. "The best we can figure out is that these two ladies somehow stole another child's birth certificate to smuggle this little one out of the country. It's really a miracle they were caught."

A smile spreads across my face as I hear my favorite word, miracle.

"We are going to try to find who the child's parents are and return him to them. How long can he stay here?"

"As long as you need," I answer. "That's what we are here for." I look down at the now sleeping baby in my arms and let out a sigh.

I pull out a folder from my file cabinet and hand the officers the required forms to sign.

"Wow. You really do have everything in top legal shape here don't you?" remarks the officer. I grin as I realize I've impressed the police. I make a photo copy of their badges and staple all the forms together. I write Leonard at the top of the papers, naming my new little boy after one of my uncles. The officers are getting ready to leave, and we all make our way back out to the playroom.

"Wait," I say. "It is our custom to pray every time a child enters these doors. Would you care to stay a few more minutes as we pray?"

The officers turn to each other and agree. We bow our

heads, and I pray that if Leonard has been kidnapped that his mother and father would be found soon. I also pray for God to comfort his parents as they must be sick with worry over their son. I pray for the two Spanish women who will be spending their first night in jail for making a very stupid decision. I pray for each of the officers. And lastly, I thank God for his sovereignty and that He has a plan for all of our lives.

The officers smile and shake my hand as they leave. One turns back and says, "This really doesn't look like an orphanage."

"Thank you," I say. "Orphanage really isn't the look I've been going for. This is just my home and these are my children."

Leonard's story made it quickly to the press. We had reporters calling continuously to interview me and photograph him. I refused the photos because I could not imagine exploiting my new baby in that way, but I agreed to the interviews. I was hoping that his birth parents would hear the news and search us out to retrieve their child. The result seriously shocked me. We received numerous phone calls from men and women claiming to be Leonard's parents. I was reminded of the scene in the movie Annie that came out in the early 80's. Annie has been raised in an orphanage and a millionaire named Mr. Warbucks takes a special interest in her story. He truly wants to find Annie's birth family, so he offers a large reward to the couple that can prove they are Annie's parents. Because of the reward, mobs of people show up claiming to be the little orphan's long lost family.

Precious Miracles was not offering any type of reward, and there weren't exactly mobs of people, but the concept was similar. I interviewed men and women for several days, each swearing they were Leonard's birth parents. I felt completely overwhelmed. How would I know who the true parents were? Why were there so many people desperate for a child, and yet I had a houseful of "unwanted" children? With my social worker and my lawyer, we devised a plan to determine who Leonard's family was. We had a specific set of questions we would ask, and we would have to do a DNA test. We obtained a court order from a judge prohibiting our releasing the child without a positive DNA match. God's guidance and comfort during this time was clearly identifiable.

When the police would drive up to our house with yet another couple, I would let them in only to the front yard but not to the house. The older children would shout with glee, "The police are here again!" I would interview the families outside and if I thought there was a possibility of them being the true family I would show them in and point them towards Leonard. Most couples never made it to the door.

Leonard had a prominent strawberry birthmark on his face, and no one ever mentioned this. One afternoon, the doorbell rang yet again, and I answered. I showed a distraught woman into the front courtyard and began to ask the routine questions. All of her details matched up with Leonard's. Then she took her index finger and traced her own face saying, "He has a birthmark right here." That was the clincher for me. I opened the door of the house. Once inside, she looked around and immediately ran to Leonard who was sitting contentedly in a bouncy chair. I hadn't needed to point him out, she had found him. I knew right then and there this was Leonard's mother. Because of the court order, it was not in my power to let her take her son home that afternoon. I told her that a DNA test would be necessary, even though I was convinced she was the true mother. She ecstatically agreed. "I'll do anything. Just tell me where to go to have it done!"

Within a few days, she had her DNA test done and I took

Leonard to get his done. Both sets of results were taken before the judge to determine the match. The judge agreed this was the mother of the child in question and signed the release form. The next day, Leonard's mother could come to pick up her son. Television crews came with her to our house to film the reuniting of the lost son and his birth mother. I felt tear drops forming in my eyes as I handed over the precious little boy. It was a bittersweet moment. Leonard had only been a part of my life for about a month, and yet, I already loved him. Of course, I was thrilled to know that he would be with his birth mother again. Leonard's mother handed him over to her husband and threw her arms around my waist and wept.

"Thank you for loving my son as if he were yours," she said. "And thank you for not letting anyone else take him from me. It would have been easier for you and less expensive to have given him away to the first person who claimed him. Thank you for waiting for me."

I returned her hug and explained loud enough for the television cameras to pick up that I had a strong faith in God. I clarified that it was God who had told me which woman was Leonard's mother. Then I handed her a gospel track with directions to our church and watched as they walked down the street to catch the bus.

17

Elsie and Edna

A Miraculous Reunion

It was 11:00 one morning, and I had been sorting through donations for our giant yard sale that weekend. Many times people would give us adult clothes or other items we were unable to utilize, and I would turn around and sell these things as a way to increase our revenue. I was busy working on this fund raising project in my office when the phone rang. I picked it up calmly and quickly distinguished the voice I heard. It was Cecilia, the social worker at For His Children. The anxiety in Cecilia's voice was apparent right away. She told me the Red Cross had just called her about a little lost girl. "They need someone to get her at once," she said frantically. "We don't really have the space, and we're reluctant to take in children that are possibly not abandoned. Is there any way that you can help out?"

"Well, let me pray about it," I started.

"They say that she needs to be picked up by noon."

"That's one hour!" I said looking at the clock on the wall.

"I know, Stacey. Please will you take this child?"

"Alright, Cecilia, I'm on it."

I hung up with Cecilia and called the Red Cross and told them that I would be there shortly to pick up the little girl. I quickly instructed my staff what to do for lunch, strapped a car seat in the back of my car, and took off towards downtown Quito.

When I arrived at the Red Cross, shelter I was given the few details about the nameless child. She was between two and three years old. She had been discovered wandering alone in an open air market place. No one at the market claimed her, and she was too young to know where her home was. The Red Cross had been contacted, and she was taken to the shelter. While at the shelter, her picture had been put in the local newspapers but no one responded to the story. The Red Cross's policy was to keep children at the shelter for only a week and the week was up. The little girl did not speak, and they didn't know her name or her exact age.

I was overcome with sadness as I thought of how scared this little girl must be among unfamiliar people. I bent down and said, "I have a pretty house with lots of children and toys. Would you like to come with me?"

She nodded her head and reached out her arms. I was struck by the willingness of this small child to go with a total stranger. She did not cry or even whimper. I quickly began filling out all the necessary forms. The line on the page where the child's name should go was noticeably and disturbingly blank. I turned to her and said, "Can I call you Elsie? My Grandmother's name is Elsie." She just looked at me. "Elsie it is!" I said with a chuckle, and I scooped her up into my arms.

There were two boys also at the shelter that day. One was nine years old and the other was eleven. "Who is taking them?" I whispered to the social worker.

"They have both run away from home," she answered apathetically. "We are trying to locate their parents also. They just came today though."

The younger of the two noticed that we were talking about them and said, "Can we go with you too? We'll be good."

I turned away quickly to hide my tears and tried to regain

my composure. "I am so sorry buddy," I said. "I have a house for babies. I have no room for big boys like you."

"She's not a baby," he said, pointing at Elsie.

"I only have cribs and baby toys," I continued to explain. "And your moms must really be missing you."

I felt like I had been hit by a bus as I walked out of that shelter, leaving those two boys behind. What would become of them? Why had they run away? Were they victims of abuse? I said a prayer for protection for them. I knew full well that Precious Miracles was not designed or able to take in older children. I was reminded that I really was not able to care for all the needy children in Quito, just the ones God had asked me to care for.

As I carried Elsie to my car, I tried to get her to speak to me. I buckled her in and she did not resist me at all. I was blown away at how compliant she was being with me, having never seen me before. I asked her different questions on the ride home and I got no response. She made no effort to talk.

When we arrived at Precious Miracles, my mom was waiting for us. We immediately began to clean Elsie up. I ran a bath for her and started removing her clothes. As I did, I was amazed at the filth on this little girl. She had a very foul odor. She had dirt all over her little body. Fleas and other insects started jumping off of her and flying around the room. I gently lowered her into the bathtub. The expression on her face told me that she had never been immersed in water before. She did not cry or struggle. She did not seem to be afraid, but rather awestruck. I splashed the water with the palm of my hand and she giggled. I gently took her hand and did the same, and she giggled again. The water was instantly black so we dumped the grimy water and refilled the tub.

The second bath produced light brown colored water, so we repeated the process one more time. After three baths she was clean. I scrubbed her little head with shampoo and as I did, realized she had a terrible case of lice. We had lice shampoo on hand, so I asked one of the staff to bring it to me. As I waited, the little bugs were running down her neck. I started crying quietly as I thought of the terrible injustice that had been done to this little child.

We scrubbed her hair with the lice shampoo several times, but it seemed that the more I scrubbed, the more nits I could see. I looked over at my mom and I said, "I think we have to shave her little head."

We had nine other children to care for, some of whom had long hair. We had stuffed animals and fuzzy blankets, and there would be no way that we could conquer this epidemic once it got out. I felt that we had no choice. So I explained to Elsie that we were going to take the yuckiness out of her hair, but that it wouldn't hurt and soon her hair would be long and pretty again.

I held Elsie, and my mom shaved her little head. She sat still and patient during the whole process. Then we smoothed lotion on her sunburned skin, put clean clothes on her and went downstairs to introduce her to the other children. As I was showing her off, she saw a trash can in the corner of the room. She bolted to it and started rummaging through the garbage looking for food. I ran after her and lifted her up into my arms. I could not stop the downpour of tears that was emerging from my eyes. "Sweet, sweet little girl," I said to her. "We have plenty of food here. I promise you right now that you will never have to look in the garbage for food again." I pulled her towards myself and rubbed her little back.

It was time for dinner, and I told the children to wash up before their meal. With the staff's help we washed all the children's hands and sat them in their chairs. I pulled a shiny new red chair to the toddler table and had Elsie sit in it. Before passing out the ham and cheese sandwiches, I had all the children bow their heads and fold their hands. They did so ritualistically.

Elsie looked around in wonder. We thanked God for our food and for our new sister.

The next morning for breakfast the routine was the same. Then at lunch when I called the children to the table, Elsie ran to the sink and turned on the water. When she got to the table, she pulled out her red chair and sat in it. No sooner had she taken her seat when she folded her hands in front of her and bowed her head. I smiled at the staff member standing there with me. Elsie had not been with us 24 hours yet, and she already knew our routine. I unsuccessfully attempted to blink back my tears as I thanked God for the food that He had provided and for the peace that He had given my sweet little Elsie who was acting as if she had always been part of our family.

Elsie warmed up more and more every day with us. It took quite a bit of effort from us to get a smile to cross her face, but we persisted. The extent of her fear at all her new surroundings, I'll never know. I can only imagine how difficult it must have been for her to be able to trust us. But she did. She quickly adapted to our routine and seemed to thrive with it. She knew that there would be three meals a day and that there would never be a lack of food. She knew she would get a bath every evening and that every night she would be warm in her own bed. Soon she was interacting with the other children and participating in our little preschool. She thoroughly enjoyed arts and crafts and was always very proud of her creations. She never attempted to speak, however, and that worried me. Little did I know all of that was about to change when the miracle continued a few months later.

Elsie had been part of our family for about three months when Cecilia from For His Children called again. She had remembered calling me several months earlier to request me taking in little Elsie. "I never heard the outcome," she started. "Did you end up taking her?"

"Yes!" I said, "And she's doing wonderfully."

She continued, "What I'm about to tell you may get confusing, so stick with me." She explained that about three months ago, FHC had also taken in a little girl about one-year old named Edna. Edna's father had willingly dropped her off at their door, saying he was unable to care for his daughter. He admitted that he and Edna's mother were drug addicts and that they needed someone to help them with the care of their child.

I was trying to figure out where Cecilia was going with all of this when she continued.

Edna's aunt had arrived at FHC to inquire on the well-being of her niece. She had been given the information by her brother-in-law, Edna's father. She herself was a widow and had four children of her own. Her intent was not to care for Edna, just to put her mind at ease that the child was being well cared for. And as she sat in Cecilia's office, she cried for her other niece, Edna's older sister that had been missing for about the same time.

Cecilia, by the miraculous intervention of God, put the pieces together and thought that maybe, just maybe the little girl from the Red Cross could be Edna's older sister. So, she called me.

"Can we come by your place with the aunt to see if she can identify your little girl?"

"Certainly!" I said. So we made the arrangements to have her come to the house the next day.

I chose not to say anything to Elsie. Because of her almost non-existent vocabulary, I wasn't sure how much she would understand. The next day, Cecilia, the psychologist of FHC, and Edna's aunt arrived at our door.

As soon as the aunt saw little Elsie, a unique mixture of sorrow, relief and pity crossed her face. "That's her!" she said. "That's my niece." Elsie in turn recognized her aunt and ran from her. I wondered if she was afraid of the aunt herself, or possibly what she represented.

I held Elsie in my lap and comforted her. I said, "No one is taking you from me, sweetheart. Your aunt wanted to see how you are doing and if you like it here with Mommy Stacey. But you don't have to go anywhere." I felt Elsie's body relax in my arms, and I knew she had understood.

The aunt did not want to stay long. She filled me in on more details about Elsie that I appreciated and then the three women left. As soon as they drove off, I called Melinda, Director of FHC. She was happy to hear that we had discovered the identity of the little girl in my home. "Well, they should be together," she said. "They're sisters. They should live together and they should go up for adoption together."

"I completely agree!" I said.

"Can you take Edna or should I take Elsie?" she asked.

"Oh no!" I nearly hollered. "After all this time getting Elsie adapted to us, you're not taking her!"

Melinda chuckled and we made plans to transition Edna to our home. They would live together as sisters, and we would start the process of looking for a family that would take both of them.

The very next afternoon, I went to FHC to pick up little Edna. She was still young enough to be quite adaptable and easy going. I drove her to my home and walked in the door. Elsie did not hear me enter. I was holding Edna in my arms when I approached Elsie. She looked up at me, then upon seeing her sister, exclaimed, "Ñaña!" which is a quichua word for "sister." The tears had formed in my eyes and were running down my cheeks so suddenly that I hadn't even felt them coming.

Edna looked at Elsie as if to say, "Hmmm you look familiar." But there was no doubt that Elsie knew and remembered her sister. Elsie flooded Edna with toys. She seemed to be saying, "This place has tons of stuff!" First, she took all the wooden blocks from a basket on the shelf. She poured the blocks onto Edna's lap. Then she removed the blocks and stacked the dolls high on top of Edna's legs. After removing the dolls, she repeated the process with the books, then the stuffed animals, and lastly the canisters of play-dough. Edna sat motionless as she watched her sister play this game. Elsie was giggling gleefully.

In spite of all the other children at Precious Miracles, Edna and Elsie maintained a particular bond together. They always knew they were sisters. This fairytale has the classic ending: Elsie and Edna truly did live happily ever after.

18

george
A Child Meets Love

A breeze blew over me, and I pulled my cardigan tighter around my torso. It was early afternoon, and I was standing outside the Quito airport. I looked up at the sign that said National Arrivals and knew I was in the right place. Just five hours earlier, I had received a phone call asking if I could take in a baby girl from Macas, a jungle city. During the brief phone call with Becky, the social worker, I was told the little girl had been abandoned by her family. She had spent the last three weeks in a Macas hospital and was now ready to be released. Because there are no orphanages in Macas, it was imperative that she be placed in Quito. When I had agreed to take in the child, Becky had flown to Macas to pick her up and bring her to me.

I anxiously inspected every woman that came out of the airport doors. I had only spoken to Becky on the phone and didn't know what she looked like. Soon a woman came up to me with a little boy in her arms.

"Are you Stacey?" she asked.

"Yes," I replied, furrowing my brow.

"I'm Becky and surprise, it's a boy!" she laughed. "We obviously had a communication error somewhere along the way. His name is George and he's about two years old."

"Wow! okay. So it's not a girl and he's not a baby? Well, that works too!" I said.

I received George into my arms and smiled down on his little face. He was silent and calm, yet appeared to be scared and confused. When we arrived at home, I realized he could barely hold himself up in a sitting position. His tummy was largely disproportionate and bloated. His little head was shaved bald revealing many scars. As I bathed him, I realized that the scars were not merely on his head but all over his tan colored body. I cringed as I thought of how severely mistreated this little boy had been in his short life.

What repercussions would his abuse have on him? Would I be able to undo the harm that had been done? Would he be able to forget his past? I put clean clothes on him, then pulled him close to me and squeezed. "I'm sorry you've been hurt. I'm going to do everything in my power to not allow that to ever happen again. You're safe here little buddy." As I released my squeeze, he looked up at my face. And then almost mechanically he put his arms around me and hugged back.

"That's right!" I said sensitively. "That's a hug, and we do a lot of that around here."

I carried him into the kitchen and placed him in a high chair. I heated up a bowl of vegetable barley soup and placed it on the tray in front of him. With one hand, he grabbed the edge of the bowl and yanked it towards himself, then wrapped his arm around the bowl. He threw the spoon on the floor, glared up at me and growled. My eyes widened and I took a step back. I was speechless. He took the bowl in both hands and poured the soup down his throat, spilling it all over the front of him in the process.

Then he slammed the empty bowl down on the tray. I walked cautiously back over to him and reached for the bowl. He grabbed it forcefully and growled again.

"I want to give you more," I said, attempting a smile. His

glare was intense. "That's okay," I continued. "We have lots of bowls." So I pulled out another bowl from the cupboard and filled it. I approached his chair warily and set the warm bowl in front of him.

He looked at me questioningly and then proceeded to gobble up the soup. We repeated this little dance until he had finished four bowls of soup. The maternal instinct in me wanted to continue to feed him, but the rational part of my brain told me that he had eaten enough, and I certainly did not want him to be ill.

After dinner, I rocked little George in my rocking chair and sang him a lullaby. He fell asleep in my arms. I gently laid him down in his crib and grabbed the large folder of papers I had received at the airport a few hours earlier. I sat on the floor next to his crib and proceeded to find out as much information as I could about the new member of my family.

As I read through the file, I felt nauseous. On the paper in plain, unmistakable Spanish were the words, 'Mother traded her son for a pig.' I read and reread the paragraph that stated those facts so clearly. George was one of many children in his home. He spent the majority of his time outdoors under his house that was built on stilts. A neighbor woman suspected abuse, and had offered George's mother a pig in exchange for him.

Unbelievably, George's mother had conceded. Upon completing the transaction, the neighbor had rushed little George to the nearest hospital in Macas, where he had been treated for severe malnourishment and anemia for almost three weeks.

I looked through the crib rails and through my tears at the peaceful little boy who lay before me. How was it possible that this precious child had been traded by his birth mother for a farm animal? The woman who brought him into this world had regarded him as no more than a swine. Then I pondered the fact that he was still so sick and weak. He could barely sit up unassisted. I could hardly imagine what he had been like three weeks prior. As I watched his little chest rise and fall with each breath, I thanked God for putting me in George's life, and for putting George in mine.

Most of us will never be able to fully comprehend this type of rejection. But Jesus Christ was rejected in a far greater way.

> *He was in the world, and the world was made through Him, and the world did not know Him. He came to His own and His own did not receive Him (Hebrews 4:14-15 John 1:10-11).*

> *Coming to Him as to a living stone rejected indeed by men, but chosen by God and precious (1 Peter 2:4).*

George too was rejected by men, but chosen by God and precious. The most amazing turn of events occurred with this child. He did not display an animal-like behavior for long. In fact, it was only three days after his arrival that I placed some corn bread on his tray, and he broke off a piece of the bread and handed it back to me. He was willing to share. In the short three day period he had realized that he was not going to go hungry in this house. In his two-year old reasoning, he had already figured out there would always be plenty of food in our home. George had learned to give of what had been given to him.

The day I met George's forever family is a highlight of my time at Precious Miracles. I sat with his new mother, Heidi, showing her the scrapbook I had prepared for them. As I turned each page, stories were sparked in my memory. I told her of the time that he had escaped our time-out playpen by tearing through the mesh side. I told her of the time that there was a chunk of wall missing from a corner where he had taken a bite. We looked at pictures of his first steps. I told her of the books he liked me to read to him. I told her of the times I rocked him in my arms and prayed for his forever family. We laughed at the humorous things. And our eyes got misty as we were both harshly aware of how much abuse and trauma this child had seen before his arrival to my home.

Our meeting was coming to an end, and the time had come to release George to his new parents. I swallowed dramatically, trying to keep my emotions under control. Heidi put her arms around me as she might have done to her lifelong friend. She held me tight and then said, "Thank you. Thank you for being the first person to love my son." The irony of that phrase is etched forever in my memory. That is why Precious Miracles was founded. Our primary objective is to love children. Many times we are the first people to show love to the children who arrive at our doors. Sometimes we love them through their crisis situation. Showing God's love to them is what we are all about, and we do so joyously until their forever families can carry on the privilege.

19

lizzy

Baby in Prison

I had taken some time off from my usual hectic schedule to do some shopping with my dad for my mom's upcoming birthday. Our afternoon had been rather unproductive, and in fact, my only purchase was the ice-cream cone I was enjoying. We turned a corner in the large three-story mall and almost ran right into a couple who was speaking English. I stepped back, and before I could utter excuse me, I heard my name.

"Stacey? Is that you?"

I smiled and nodded, seeing my third grade school teacher. "How are you, Mrs. Ewan? It's nice to see you again."

"You can call me Joan," she said laughing. "I heard you started an orphanage here. Is that true?"

"It is true," I affirmed, still nodding.

"Wow! This is great. I have a dilemma that I think you can help me with. I have a ministry in the women's prison here in Quito. Did you know that? I do Bible studies with a group of foreign girls who only speak English. One of our girls, from Indonesia, is pregnant. She got pregnant in prison and she wants to give up her baby for adoption.

What can we do?"

I quickly explained the procedures of adoption. The Ecuadorian laws did not allow for direct adoption. This meant that all abandoned or orphaned children were required to go to an orphanage or institution until they were assigned to an adoptive family. I assured Joan that Precious Miracles would be happy to be the baby's transitional home. I was anxious to get back to my house to start dinner, so we quickly made arrangements to meet at the women's prison the next Wednesday. That way I could meet Kimmie, the Indonesian girl, myself and we could discuss her baby's future.

On Wednesday morning, I met Joan outside the intimidating walls of the prison. I had not returned since my episode with Sarah months earlier. We went in together, and I was astounded at the respect Joan received from the guards and inmates. It was a completely different environment with her by my side. She took me up to Kimmie's room and introduced us. I explained who I was and what I did. We spoke for about an hour, going back and forth between her broken English and her newly learned Spanish. We both had scores of questions. I asked about her certainty of giving up her child. I asked about her extended family, her sentence, and her plans for returning to her home country. She told me she was positive she did not want to raise a baby in the environment in which she currently found herself. Her sentence for drug trafficking was eight years, and she had not finished even her first year yet. She shook her head as she acknowledged that prison was no place for a child to spend his first years of life. She stated that when she was released she planned on returning to Indonesia. Her child's father was black, and her half-black child would not be accepted by her family back home. She was completely certain that she needed an alternative to raising her own child.

I asked for more details about the child's father. She explained that he had been visiting his own mother in prison and through his repeated visits, Kimmie had formed a relationship with him. He had become physically abusive, however, and she did not want him to have custody of the child or even to know the baby's whereabouts. She had already asked for a restraining order against him prohibiting his entry into the jail.

Child custody in Ecuador is very different than it is in the United States. A father will almost never get awarded custody of his children in a custody battle. If the mother does not wish for him to see the children, the courts almost always rule in her favor. I explained all this to Kimmie to reassure her that I did not think he could complicate the issue.

"Oh you don't know him," she argued. "He can complicate the issue if he wants to complicate the issue."

Not fully understanding what she meant, I continued. "It would be difficult for him to even prove he was the father, as DNA tests are rare and expensive. And most likely he would have no desire to prove he was the father, as this would imply his paying child support. If you have a restraining order against him, it is implied that your baby is also protected by that order."

After praying together, I asked her if I could give her a hug. She consented and I wrapped my arms around her. I wrote down my cell phone number and told her to call me if she had any questions, doubts, or if there was anything I could bring to her.

The months passed and the precious miracle inside of Kimmie continued to grow and develop. The baby's father did not disappear as I had hoped he would. He called the jail threatening Kimmie's life. He told her that he would take the child from her when it was born. He said he would find out through other women at the prison when she left for the hospital, and he would wait for her there to steal the baby. When asked why he wanted the baby, he told her he planned on selling it. Kimmie had no way to run away from him.

He had managed to come into the prison, in spite of his restraining order, by bribing the guards. When he did, she would run up to her room and lock herself inside.

I visited Kimmie regularly, always joining Joan for Wednesday Bible study. I was even privileged to prepare and give the Bible study on a few occasions. I brought Kimmie prenatal vitamins, maternity clothes and milk. She confided in me about her fear of what the father of her child would be capable. Every visit, we would end in prayer and I would plead with God to protect Kimmie and her unborn baby. "We won't tell him anything about me, alright?" I told Kimmie. "When your baby is born, I will come to the hospital with you. Then I will take your baby home with me and the father never has to know who has the child."

The night arrived in which I received the call from the maternity hospital. The voice on the other line told me that Kimmie was there and about to deliver her child. It was late at night, and I debated driving over there. The maternity hospital was in a dangerous part of town, and going anywhere alone at night was not wise. My heart went out to Kimmie giving birth all by herself, and I put my selfish fears aside. I got in my car and drove to accompany her immediately. Once inside the hospital, I was yelled at, pushed, and bumped into as I made my way to find Kimmie. I finally did find her and she was still in labor. She looked up at me with appreciation.

"Thank you for coming Stacey," she cried. "I'm so scared."

I smiled as I sat next to her and grabbed her hand. Her contractions were getting closer and closer together, and soon I was forced to leave her room. I was told I had to leave the hospital and that I could return the next day during visiting hours. I prayed quickly with Kimmie and left.

The next day, as promised, I returned to the hospital during the allotted time. The conditions of that hospital have made an indelible print in my memory. I had never seen anything like it before. On the third, floor in one enormous room, lay rows of young women on hospital cots no wider than the girls themselves. There were four rows with about 25 beds in each row. The beds were close together, allowing just enough room for a person to stand between them. The first row of women had the heads of their beds up against the wall. The second row was facing the opposite direction, and between the first and second row was about three feet of space. The third row's heads almost touched those of the second row, and between the third and fourth row there was another three feet of space. The nurses had babies literally stacked on carts that I was sure were created for transporting food. The nurses would roll these carts down the three foot aisles between the ladies and hand a baby systematically to each woman. As I stood next to Kimmie's bed, I was flabbergasted. "How do they know they are giving the right child to the right mother?" I exclaimed.

The women were given about 40 minutes with their newborns, and then the carts were wheeled around again to pile the children up again and return them to the nursery.

Soon, Kimmie's baby girl was handed to her. As she nursed her infant, I asked if she had a name picked out for her daughter. She said she hadn't thought of a name, and I asked her if we could call her Lizzy after my niece. She agreed. When little Lizzy had finished eating, I asked to hold her. I picked her up and stared into her beautiful little eyes. She was a gorgeous baby girl. As I sat mesmerized, there was some commotion in the hall just a few feet away from us. I looked up and saw a very large man trying to push back the guards. He was yelling, "That's my child! Give me my child!" My heart pounded as I met Kimmie's gaze.

"Is that him?" I asked. I had never seen Lizzy's father before.

Kimmie sat straight up in her tiny bed and said with a shaky voice, "Yes. That's him.

How did he know my baby was born? How did he find me?"

I sat next to her and stroked her hand. "It'll be all right," I said, trying to convince myself just as much as her. Men were not allowed in the room without permission and he was escorted out. We were all a bit shaky from the ordeal.

Visiting hours were over, and I found out from the doctor that she would be released the next day back to the prison. I made arrangements to meet Kimmie at the front of the hospital the next morning where I would take the baby for her. That night, Kimmie called me at my home. She said that she had received a message from the father. He had sent in a letter with a nurse. The letter said that he would retrieve his baby no matter what. He was not afraid of killing the white girl to get his child. My heart dropped. My life was being threatened by a man that was easily 150 pounds heavier than me and completely capable of hurting me. I already loved Lizzy with all my heart. Would I risk my life to save hers? The next day, I disguised myself as best as I could. It was the first time I could ever remember truly fearing for my life. My dad and my social worker came with me to the hospital. My dad drove his car. When we arrived at the hospital, Kimmie and Lizzy had already been released. They were back in prison. We rushed over to the prison. The guards let Kimmie come out to the front gate with her baby. My dad stayed in the car watching to see if he saw anyone hanging around the prison walls. Kimmie kissed her child and said to me, as tears gathered in the corners of her eyes, "Please take good care of my baby. Please protect her. Please love her."

I hugged her tight and assured her that I would do the things she was asking of me. We explained our situation to the prison guards. I put little Lizzy inside my sweatshirt and was escorted by two armed guards out of the prison. I looked all around me and saw no one. My dad was waiting right outside with the car running. I jumped inside and we sped off. I put Lizzy in the car seat as we drove down the street. Dad took a long detour home, and we checked behind us the entire time to see if we were being followed. It did not seem that we were.

We arrived at Precious Miracles with our new bundle of

love and showed her off to the excited children who had been waiting for us. As I sat and held my beautiful infant in my arms, I felt an immeasurable love overwhelm me. I looked down at her and I whispered, "I really would have given up my life to protect you Lizzy. You're worth it to me." I thanked God for this little life with which I had been entrusted. I prayed for her safety while at Precious Miracles.

Lizzy's father never did find her. He sent many threatening messages to Kimmie in prison but he never discovered his child's whereabouts, and after several months we stopped worrying. We were sure he had given up and we were safe. I never heard from or saw that man again, and neither did Kimmie.

After nine months, Kimmie changed her mind and requested that we return her daughter to her. We filed the necessary paperwork and broken hearted, sent Lizzy to live with her mother in jail. It didn't last long, and Kimmie was calling me sobbing. "I can't do this!" she cried. "Please take my daughter to live with you again!"

"Kimmie," I said harshly. "This is not a game. If you want us to care for Lizzy we will be happy to do so, but you have to make up your mind. The differences between my house and the jail are astronomical, and we can't assume that Lizzy doesn't notice or isn't affected by the change in environments."

Kimmie agreed that she would send her daughter to us and that this time it would be for real. She would not attempt to take her daughter back again. Her promise was not kept.

Shortly after Lizzy's first birthday, Kimmie angrily demanded that we return her daughter. I felt like my heart was in a million pieces when I said, "Kimmie this is it. If you take Lizzy back to live with you, I can't help you anymore."

"I'm so alone. I miss her," was all Kimmie could say.

So again, we procedurally filled out the papers. When it came right down to it, I couldn't stop loving and helping Lizzy. I had grown attached to her, and I still wanted to do anything possible for her. I visited Lizzy frequently and always brought her clothes, medicines, and toys. One day, Kimmie called sobbing.

"Kimmie, I was serious," I started. "I cannot take your child back home with me for a third time."

"No, Stacey it's not that!" she cried. "The inmates are rioting and protesting and Lizzy needs milk. I can't get any milk for her. Can you please bring me some?"

Without a second thought I agreed and ran to the grocery store. After picking up a few liters of milk, I made my way to the prison. I got there and noticed there were TV camera crews outside. I hid my purse under the seat of the car, grabbed my grocery sack and knocked on the giant metal gate. The little porthole was opened and the guard said, "What?"

"Good morning," I said. "I've come to give some milk to the daughter of Kimmie Hotisam. I have no desire to enter. I can just pass it through here…" I was cut off by the porthole being slammed shut and the giant gate was opened. The guard grabbed my arm and flung me inside.

"Wait!" I said. "I didn't mean to come in. I know something is not right with the riots, and the TV cameras. I just wanted to make sure that little Lizzy Hotisam got this milk."

The guard threw his head back and laughed. "Hey girls," he shouted in the direction of the office. Out walked three women guards. "Get a load of this! This gringa came here to give one of the inmates' baby some milk!"

They were all laughing, and I demanded to know what the problem was. They explained that two days earlier the inmates had gone on strike. They had some guards in their cells as hostages. When the news teams came to report on the story, they had taken them hostage too.

"How can they take hostages?" I asked innocently.

"They have knives and guns!" answered the guard, patronizingly.

"Oh okay," I said trying to sound calm. "I had no idea. The milk can't be that big of a deal. I'll just leave."

The four guards roared with laughter again. "Like !%$@ you will! You're in here now. You're not leaving!"

I felt my heart start to race. "No, I'm serious. Just let me go right back out," I said, motioning to the gate I had just walked through. I felt tears forming in my eyes, and I was angry at my physical response. I didn't want to cry! A man dressed in a suit came out of the office. "What's going on here?" he asked. He was one of the social workers that handled the prisoner's cases.

"I used to be a foster mom for Lizzy Hotisam," I explained. "Kimmie, her mother called me today requesting milk. I had no idea there were riots going on, and I just came to bring a baby some milk." At my last words, I lifted up my grocery bag to show him. "But now the guards say that I can't leave and that I'm going to be taken hostage."

"You idiots!" screamed the social worker at the guards. "Why does it still give you so much pleasure to harass people?" Then turning to me he said, "We can go through the kitchen, and you can hand the boxes of milk through a window. The inmates can't reach you in the kitchen."

"Okay," I said, my voice still shaky.

The social worker escorted me to the kitchen. The filthy room had not been used since the riots started. There were tiny windows at the very top of the wall that looked into the main courtyard. I stepped up on the counter to look through. No one could see me, but I could see the chaos below. I saw the screaming inmates and the terrified journalists hovering in a corner. As I searched the mob, I saw one of the girls from the Wednesday Bible studies. "Zoe," I screamed. She turned, looking all around her. "Up here, in the kitchen!"

She caught my eye and said, "Stacey? What are you doing here?"

"Oh I'm so foolish, Zoe." I said. "Kimmie asked me to bring Lizzy milk, and I didn't know all of this was happening. Can you take her the milk?"

"Sure, but then you need to get out of here. You're not safe here!"

"I know, I know." I said. "Here's the milk." I squeezed the cartons through the small window, thanked Zoe and climbed off the counter. Once back out in the front of the prison, the social worker convinced the guards to let me go. I thanked him for being so kind and helpful to me and nearly ran out of the open metal gate.

Back at home, I told the employees my day's adventure and we laughed. I realized how easily my day could have taken a major turn for the worse, and I thanked God for His protection in spite of my imprudence.

I continued to visit Lizzy and Kimmie, making sure to watch the local news before I made the trip over to the prison. Joan left Ecuador shortly after and interestingly enough, my mom took over the prison ministry. Every year on Lizzy's birthday, I went in to get her and take her back to my house where we threw her a birthday party. We did other activities as well to give her a taste of the real world outside the prison walls.

Kimmie's sentence was shortened, and just after Lizzy's fourth birthday they were both on a plane back to Indonesia.

20

israel

Heaven is a Little Brighter

From the moment little Israel was brought into this world and long after he was taken from it, he experienced adversity. Israel was born to alcoholic parents.

I am not referring to people who drink occasionally or fail to know when they have had enough. I'm referring to people who day in and day out live in a total stupor, people who do not know what day of the week it is, or even if it is day or night, and people who live in filth and constant hunger because every cent they obtain goes to buy more alcohol.

Israel was conceived in drunkenness, and during his entire time in utero was exposed to the effects of alcohol. Israel had fetal alcohol syndrome and severe cerebral palsy among other undiagnosed medical problems. He had no motor control over any part of his body except his facial expressions. Israel would be fed seldom, and as a result was severely malnourished and underdeveloped. Many times he would be given alcohol to quiet his incessant cries for help.

Israel's mother and father remained in a perpetual state of drunkenness. When the alcohol would run out and their bodies would attain temporary sobriety, they would use their sick little boy to beg on the streets. Walking between cars parked at stop lights, they would hold up their handicapped son to increase their earnings. This proved profitable for them, and they made quite a bit of money exploiting him.

Israel and his parents lived in the slums of south Quito. Their dwelling was essentially no more than a room with one small window and a metal door. Rachel lived in the adjacent room in the barrio with her own children. She saw Israel occasionally and heard his cries frequently. Many times she would walk over to her neighbor's dwelling to peek in their windows. She would often see Israel lying on the floor and crying while his intoxicated parents were passed out beside him. He was starving. He was being severely neglected. Israel's survival can only be attributed to a supernatural act of God.

Rachel could not stand to see a child suffer this greatly and chose to call the police. She described the situation and gave the location. The police assured her that they would check on the situation, but they never came. She called again, and again never giving up hope that someday, someone would pay attention to this child and rescue him from his situation. Finally after much insistence, the police came to the address. There the officers could see for themselves a small disabled child crying on the floor. His inebriated parents lay next to him unaware.

The officers immediately removed Israel from his house and took him to the largest Catholic orphanage in Quito. His parents did not wake up or notice their child was being taken from them. The same afternoon of Israel's arrival at the orphanage, I received a phone call. The orphanage was overcrowded and understaffed, and they felt there was no way that they could adequately care for this very special needs child. I assured them I would arrive in the morning.

I made my way across town to the orphanage, completely unprepared for the little boy I would encounter there. He was lethargic and floppy in the caregiver's arms. He could scarcely keep his eyes open, and his whole being exuded sadness and misery. I took him from the caregiver and held him close to me. I looked down into his gloomy eyes and said, "Do you want me to be your new Mommy? Do you want to come home with me?" He looked up and met my gaze, and then he smiled. Soon, that same smile would captivate everyone who came in contact with this precious miracle. It was a smile I would never be able to forget.

I carried Israel home in the back seat of a taxi cab, and he was welcomed with squeals, laughter and kisses from the other children. We prayed over Israel and asked for God's will to be done in his life.

I had the custom of giving all the children nicknames. I remember mulling over in my head, what would be a good way to shorten Israel? I was unable to come up with one.

Shortly after Israel's arrival to my home, some of my extended family was visiting us in Ecuador. My aunt Susie had accompanied my mom over to the house to meet our new miracle. His toothy smile was truly breath-taking, and my mom laughed and said affectionately, "He looks like a little chipmunk."

My aunt said, "He does! You should nickname him Chip." And just like that, his new nickname was Chip.

Israel was a truly incredible child. In spite of his many health problems, he brought so much joy to everyone around him. He loved to get personal attention and to be in the spotlight. He loved to perform and have all eyes on him. I am convinced that he was in denial that he lived with 10 other children. In his mind he was an only child. When visitors came to tour Precious Miracles, the other children would shy away. Israel, on the other hand, was the most welcoming to our company, and his trademark smile would cause even the most stoic of guests to melt. His laughter was contagious and he lit up our home.

Israel had been with us for three years. He had learned to eat very well and was growing slowly but surely. He received physical therapy three times a week, including hippotherapy every Friday. Israel had developed and thrived beyond anyone's expectations.

Then disease struck the Precious Miracles home. The sequence began with a round of chicken pox. Since this was our third occurrence with the chicken pox virus, we managed quite well. Shortly after the children recovered, we were hit with rotavirus.

Unlike chicken pox, one can get rotavirus repeatedly. It circled through our home for weeks. By the time some of the children would recuperate, others had contracted it. The vicious cycle continued. I cried every night seeing all the children in such weak and miserable conditions. By the grace of God neither the staff nor I ever caught this horrible disease.

The children's health slowly began to improve. Finally we were to the point where I was sure we had overcome the nightmare. The children were laughing and playing again.

Their fevers were down and their symptoms were gone. Israel, however, was not back to his normal chipper self. His symptoms were gone, but he seemed sluggish and his smiles were few and far between.

One night, I was startled awake by the sound of my phone ringing. My only extension was in the kitchen and I ran to answer. As I made my way down the hall, my stomach churned. A wave of sadness came over me and I instantly thought, "It's Chip. Chip is gone." I picked up the receiver.

"Hello?" I said.

"Miss Stacey!" shrieked Isabel on the other end. "Israel fainted. We can't get him to respond."

"Fainted?" I asked. "What do you mean?"

"He won't wake up!" she cried.

"Call an ambulance, I'm on my way." I said.

"We already called the ambulance." She stuttered, and with that the conversation ended.

I flew out the door and into my car and as I did, an indescribable peace came over me. I heard God say to me, "My sweet child, it does not matter how quickly you get there. Israel is with me already." I felt a mixture of emotions.

A part of me wanted to yell back, "No! Don't take him yet." Another part of me felt an overwhelming sense of joy that Israel was better now. Still another part of me felt failure.

It is my duty to keep these children safe from harm. Now I have let one go. What could I have done differently? How could this have been avoided? As these thoughts jumbled their way through my brain, I realized I was at the Precious Miracles house. There in front was an ambulance. I rushed to the door of the house and I heard Ruth, the other staff member on duty, yell to me.

"We're in here Miss Stacey!"

I ran over to the ambulance. Ruth had little Chip in her arms and two emergency personnel were working on him. The one turned to me and asked who I was.

"I'm the child's mother," I responded.

She shot her coworker a questioning glance and Ruth quickly defended my position.

"She is the child's mother." No sooner were the words out of her mouth than the male doctor shook his head and said, "He's dead. I'm so sorry but there is nothing more that I can do."

The next afternoon we held a small service for Israel, and I was touched by how many people came to pay their respects. Tears were shed, but the mood was not one of despair. Everyone there was convinced beyond a shadow of a doubt that Israel was healed. He was in heaven with a new, perfect body, and we all had a strong sense of relief at the thought.

I wish I could say that Israel's story stops there. But as I said at the beginning, we experienced adversity long after he left this world. Nearly two years after Israel's home- going, an investigation was begun. Israel's adoption papers had not been removed from the system, and someone had finally stumbled on them. This of course means that if he had still been alive, he would have been seven years old before he was considered adoptable—a tragedy in and of itself.

When the judge declared Israel adoptable, the foundation's lawyer, Dr. Palacios informed him that the child was deceased. Hearing this, the judge became irate. He immediately set forth to investigate why the child had died under Precious Miracles custody. He suspected foul play and blamed the staff (and specifically me as the Director) of intentionally harming the child. He went on to say that we had deliberately caused Israel's death.

When I heard the news, I was devastated. I had loved Israel so deeply that it was inconceivable that someone would accuse me of hurting him and so much more. I felt infuriated at the accusation. I wanted to shout at the judge, "Why did I agree to take him in? I was under no obligation to accept him from the Catholic orphanage. Why had I cared for him for three years? If I had wanted to rid myself of the child, why would I have waited so long?" I thought of all the photos and video of Israel that I had. He was happily smiling in every single one. How could they explain his happiness if he was being mistreated? My body shook with my sobs. Then I stopped. With the back of my hand, I wiped the tears from my face and took my Bible off the shelf. I read the following verses:

> *What then shall we say to these things? If God is for us who can be against us? Who shall bring a charge against God's elect? It is God who justifies* (Romans 8:31, 33).

> *Therefore humble yourselves under the mighty hand of God, that He may exalt you in due time, casting all your care upon Him, for he cares for you. Be sober, be vigilant; because your adversary the devil walks about like a roaring lion, seeking whom he may devour. Resist him, steadfast in the faith, knowing that the same sufferings are experienced by your brotherhood in the world. But may the God of all grace, who called us to His eternal glory by Christ*

Jesus, after you have suffered a while, perfect, establish, strengthen, and settle you (1 Peter 5:6-10).

When my anxious thoughts multiply within me, Your consolations delight my soul (Psalm 94:19).

For the Lord your God is God of gods and Lord of lords, the great God, mighty and awesome, who shows no partiality nor takes a bribe. He administers justice for the fatherless... (Deuteronomy 10:17).

And just like many times before, the threats were just that: threats. No harm came to me, the staff or the children as a result of this trial. And God had indeed strengthened and settled me.

21

jenny
gone!

"I just can't do it anymore!" cried the young female voice on the other end of the phone. "I've tried for almost two years, but I can't give my daughter a good life on my own. I want her to have the things I never had. I want her to be properly cared for, and I just can't..." Monica's voice trailed off.

I grabbed a tissue from the box on my desk for my eyes, and said, "That's why Precious Miracles exists. Let me give you directions to get here. Can you be here tomorrow?"

"I can come right now!" she said. "I'm in Tena though."

Tena is a city in the jungle province of Napo and easily eight hours or more from Quito.

It was mid afternoon, and the thought of this young mother and her child on a bus all night did not settle well with me.

"No," I answered. "Leave first thing in the morning. You'll be here about this time tomorrow." I proceeded to give her directions to our house. Never before had I given our home address to a birth mother. I usually met them where they were. But I knew it would be impossible for me to go to Tena. I honestly did not think twice about it. It would be good for her to come see the home and be confident that her child would be well cared for in this place.

The next day right on schedule Monica arrived at our door

with a chubby cheeked, curious little girl with cute braids coming out of the top of her head. I shook Monica's hand and welcomed her. "What's her name?" I asked.

"Jenny," she replied.

I knelt down and offered my hand to Jenny. "Welcome to my house, Jenny. Would you like to meet some friends?"

Jenny stared at me and then smiled and took my hand. We went inside, as I eagerly introduced my children to Jenny.

"Mommy," Jacob said, "Is she going to live here with me?"

"Yes, Jacob." I answered. "Jenny has come to stay with us for awhile."

In my office my social worker discussed the situation with Monica. She asked her multiple times if she was sure of her decision. Monica was crying as she stated that she had been severely abused as a child. She said she was afraid she would abuse Jenny.

She claimed to be practically homeless, an orphan herself, and she did not want Jenny to grow up in that type of environment. She assured both of us that this was the best decision and that she knew her daughter would be better off in our home and soon in an adoptive family. With a tearful goodbye she walked out of our house and presumably out of her daughter's life.

One week after Jenny's arrival she gave us quite a scare. We discovered the hard way that Jenny had dyspnea, a breathing difficulty that in its extreme form results in loss of consciousness. After throwing what seemed like a tantrum during lunch time Jenny stopped breathing. She was rushed to the hospital and by the grace of God survived the episode.

Three weeks after Monica had seemingly left her child permanently with us, she returned saying she had changed her mind. She desired to take Jenny back and give mothering another shot. Four days later Monica and I met at the attorney's office and filled out the necessary documents. Jenny had already been registered as an abandoned child and as a member of our home. If she was not in our home during one of the routine checks the ministry of social welfare carried out, the foundation would be in extreme trouble. The attorney gave Monica a difficult time, telling her that she could not treat this situation as a game. He asked her over and over again if she knew what she was doing.

Weeping, Monica said that she did. She missed her little girl and was miserable without her. After the last paper was signed, Monica accompanied me back to the Precious Miracles house. I watched as Monica once again walked out of our house and presumably out of our lives.

The story does not stop there, however. Two days after the second departure Monica and Jenny were back at the Precious Miracles front door. Monica begged me to take Jenny again. She said this time it would only be for three days. She needed to go back to Tena, and Jenny was sick and she pleaded for me to do her this favor. I brought Monica back into my office and asked her to think rationally. I reminded her that Precious Miracles was not a free day care center. As I was talking, I saw little Jenny lying limp in her mother's arms. I reached out to touch her forehead and discovered she was burning up with fever. Compassion overcame me. Although my mind was telling me not to agree to take Jenny back, I caved. Legally I knew that it would be better for me to send both girls on their way and wash my hands of the entire situation. But I loved Jenny already, and there was no guarantee of her mother's wisdom in caring for her in her sickness.

As Monica walked out of my house for the third time, she assured me she would be back in three days to retrieve her daughter. She did not return in the promised three days. After a week of not hearing from her, I followed legal procedure and started the abandonment paperwork again on Jenny. Just as claiming a child I did not have was illegal, equally dangerous for the foundation was to have a child I had not legally claimed. If the ministry of social welfare came and saw that I had a child in my care that I had not registered, I could face serious consequences. I had no choice but to register Jenny as being abandoned by her mother.

When Monica did come back, a month after her promised return, she hysterically demanded her child. I explained that because I had not even received a phone call I had been forced to assume that she had abandoned her daughter with me. I did not allow her entrance to the home and she stood in the streets screaming. As neighbors and other people passed by, she swore loudly, claiming that Precious Miracles was an illegal compound of stolen children.

I did my best to explain the situation to Monica. I assured her that she could have her daughter back if she followed the necessary protocol. She needed to appear before a judge to explain her situation and ask for the legal return of her daughter. It was not a complicated course of action and it was completely free of charge. I repeatedly told her that it was not my intent to keep Jenny from her. I explained that I would be in an extreme legal predicament if I handed Jenny over to her without the necessary documents.

Monica called incessantly, threatening me, using profanities, and insulting me. She also filed two law suits against me and I remained in a constant state of fear and anxiety. I was unable to sleep and the stress of the situation incredibly affected my emotions. I had never experienced such difficulty or animosity from a parent in the years that I had been directing Precious Miracles. Both law suits were dismissed, as the judges in each case could see that I had done nothing illegal.

Then the night came when I was awakened up by the ring of my phone. I sat straight up in bed and looked at the clock. It was 1:00 a.m. Panic swept over me as I thought of the phone call exactly a week earlier that had stated that Israel had passed away. "Who is it now Lord?!" I cried. "Have you taken another child from me?"

I ran to the phone where I heard the terror in Eloisa's voice. "We can't find Jenny," she cried. "She's not in her crib and we've looked everywhere for her."

My first reaction was frustration. What did they mean they couldn't find Jenny? How dare they wake me up for that? I asked them to give me more details, and Eloisa's voice cracked as she said, "Could you please come here, Miss Stacey?"

I pulled on some clothes and drove over to the house. Every night there were two employees doing the graveyard shift. The two women were responsible for any night feedings of the infants, caring for the most difficult special needs children who had no regular sleep schedule, and cleaning and disinfecting the house.

When I arrived at the house, the two employees explained the situation. Eloisa told me that she had vacuumed Jenny's room about an hour earlier, and she knew that Jenny was in her crib at that time. When she went to do the rounds 45 minutes later, she noticed that Jenny was no longer in her crib. As Eloisa talked, I walked around the house. I went straight for the crib and noticed that the rails were still up. It would be nearly impossible for little Jenny to climb over them without hurting herself. We checked under all 13 cribs and opened the closet doors. We looked in the three bath tubs and under the sofa and chairs in the living room. I felt short of breath as my mind raced.

Where could she be? In the stillness, I was painfully aware that my heart was pounding in my chest. It was so loud that my ears throbbed and my chest hurt. Tears rolled down my cheeks as I called out Jenny's name. I even opened the refrigerator, the oven and the dryer to look for her. After turning the house upside down, I crashed into the chair in the living room. I turned to both employees and bawled.

"Do you guys think it's possible that someone entered the house and took her?" I asked, not wanting to hear confirmation. We all agreed that was the only explanation. I called the police and we waited in anguish for them to arrive. While we waited, we tried to figure out how someone had broken in without being noticed. Eloisa said that she had gone outside to feed the dog and had not locked the front door when she came back inside. She had been vacuuming in the other bedroom, and Isabel had gone to use the restroom on the other side of the house. We determined that in those precise minutes, someone had entered and taken Jenny.

When the police arrived instead of being helpful and reassuring, they were hateful and offensive. They accused all three of us of being failures at our jobs. "You're here to save and protect children?" asked one of the officers sarcastically. "Fantastic job you're doing!" I explained that the mother of the girl that was missing had threatened us and that I was certain she had perpetrated the crime. "The crime?" the officer asked. "The only crime here is that you hold children against their parents' wishes and then allow them to be kidnapped. The only criminal here is you."

At their hateful words, my knees buckled. I sat down on the floor in despair. The police officers soon left, and I stayed at Precious Miracles the rest of the night. I was afraid to go back to my apartment alone. Was Monica done now that she had what she wanted or was this just the beginning? When the sun came up and the other children had awakened and been dressed, I brought them all into the playroom and we sat in a circle on the rug. I told them that Jenny had left the night before, and that we were going to pray for her. We took turns praying for Jenny's safety. I asked God to surround the Precious Miracles home with a hedge of protection. I asked for an extra helping of guardian angels. I prayed that Monica would leave us alone and that my children would be safe from harm.

As I prayed, I also thanked God that it had not been a worse situation. I believe it was God's providence that kept both employees on opposites sides of the house at that moment. I am almost positive, whoever came in had weapons, and they would have used them if they thought it was necessary. I thanked God that my employees had not been harmed and that the other 12 children had not been harmed.

After the prayer and making sure breakfast was underway, I called my parents. My dad graciously accompanied me to three different police stations and two courts, as we filed a missing children's report, a restraining order, and a law suit against Monica for kidnapping. Between hearings, I called our attorney and asked for his advice. I was blessed that he and all the different officers we came in contact with that day saw me as the innocent party. No one else reacted like the officers of the night before. Everyone assured me that the crime had been committed against me and against our foundation, and that neither I nor the foundation was responsible.

A week after the kidnapping, a man called claiming to be Monica's brother. He quickly stated that Jenny was fine in the care of her mother. He told me that after finding out what his sister had done, he felt deeply sorry for me and how concerned I must be. He said he just wanted to call to let me know that Monica did in fact do the kidnapping and that Jenny was fine. I thanked him profusely for his call and he hung up the phone.

I often think of Jenny. I wonder if she has had more episodes of dyspnea and if so, how Monica has handled them. I wonder if she is being well cared for and if she is happy.

When I feel discouraged, I remember that God is infinitely sovereign. He had a reason for putting Jenny in our home, and he allowed her to be taken from it. And I remember that even when I can't see the miracles that have left my care, He still sees them. No matter how far they go from me, they can never leave God's sight.

22

emilio
A Miraculous Survival

*P*raise the Lord! Praise O servants of the Lord, Praise the name of the Lord! Blessed be the name of the Lord from this time forth and forevermore! From the rising of the sun to its going down the Lord's name is to be praised. The Lord is high above all the nations, His glory above the heavens, Who is like the Lord our God, who dwells on high? Who humbles Himself to behold the things that are in the heavens and in the earth? He raises the poor out of the dust, and lifts the needy out of the ash heap, That He may seat him with princes, with the princes of His people (Psalm 113: 1-8).

Crystal set the silverware on the napkins at the two place settings, then poured the steamy black coffee in the two ceramic mugs. It was early Wednesday morning. Her employers walked into the kitchen and she politely greeted them. "Good Morning Mr. Villarreal. Good Morning Mrs. Villarreal."

She waited for them to take their seats, and then placed their breakfast plates on the table in front of them.

"Crystal," said Mrs. Villarreal. "Don't forget today is garbage pickup day."

"Yes ma'am," said Crystal as she pulled the large bag from

the long canister in the corner. She routinely tied it up and went to collect the bags from the other trash cans in the house. Crystal had been a live-in maid for the Villarreal family for many years. She didn't mind her job. Her employers were kind to her. They were a middle aged couple who didn't have children of their own, and sometimes she felt as though she was treated like a daughter. A smile spread across her face as she thought of how fortunate she was to be employed. Many of her relatives were unable to find any type of work.

Times were difficult, especially for those who didn't have a secure job.

She made her way outside to the street with all the trash bags. She shook open the large black bag in her hand in order to condense the small bags into it. Most of the neighbors already had their bags out. On garbage pickup days, everyone in the neighborhood would combine their trash to help the sanitation workers. On the corner of the two streets a large pile would form, and the sanitation workers would only have to make one stop to collect it.

As she lobbed her bag on top of the pile, she heard a noise. "That must have been my imagination," she thought. But she heard it again. It sounded like a cry. Her first thought was that there was a cat under the bags. She lifted her bag off the pile and separated the bags to find the poor animal. Not finding anything, she continued to remove the bags and the sound became louder and clearer. It was not a cat. The sound she was hearing was unmistakably that of an infant. Her hands were shaking intensely as she followed the noise and found a baby in a tied up plastic bag. She screamed and ripped open the bag. Amazingly, he was still alive. He had no clothes, and she pressed him up against her body and bolted back to the house.

"Mrs. Villarreal! Mrs. Villarreal!" she screamed.

"For goodness sake Crystal, what is it?" Mrs. Villarreal stopped dead in her tracks as she saw what Crystal was holding.

"He was in the garbage, Ma'am! Someone threw him away!" Tears were pouring relentlessly from her eyes and she sat down on the kitchen chair.

Mrs. Villarreal was trying to make sense of the events that were unfolding in front of her.

Someone had thrown away an infant? What does one do when one finds an infant in the garbage? Her husband had just left for work, so she picked up the phone and called him on his mobile.

"Did I forget something?" he answered.

"Emilio, you're never going to believe what just happened," she cried.

"What is it dear?" Mr. Villarreal asked, sensing the panic in his wife's voice.

"Crystal was throwing out our garbage and she found a baby! What do I do?"

"A baby?! Are you sure?"

"Yes I'm sure!" she nearly screamed. "She's holding him in her arms right now."

"I've heard of cases like this in the news," he said ponderingly. "You're going to have to call the police. They'll know what to do."

Mrs. Villarreal hung up the phone and told Crystal to get in the car. She decided she would go to the nearby children's hospital to leave the child there. By now, Crystal had pulled a towel from the linen closet and had the little boy wrapped up in it. She climbed in the back seat of the car holding, her precious bundle next to her. On the way to the hospital, they stopped at a drug store to buy a can of formula, bottled water and a baby bottle. They quickly prepared the milk and the baby gulped down the much needed nourishment.

At the hospital, the two women hastily found the social work office and knocked on the door. As succinctly as she was able, Mrs. Villarreal explained the morning's events to the social worker who greeted them.

"We'll admit the baby to make sure that he is alright," said the social worker. "And then we will find an institution that can take him in. You did the right thing in bringing him to us."

Mrs. Villarreal sighed with relief as she let her small frame sink into the chair. "What will become of this baby?" she asked.

"He will go to an orphanage, and then he will go up for adoption," replied the social worker.

Mrs. Villarreal thought of how many times she had discussed adoption with her husband in years prior. They had tried for many years to conceive and were never able to do so.

Her desire to be a mother was so great that she had attempted to convince her husband that they should adopt. He had never felt comfortable with the idea of being a father to a child that was not his own flesh and blood and had been adamantly against the idea.

Now it was too late. They were too old to become parents now. Why had God brought this little baby into her life too late? "Ma'am? Did you hear me?" said the social worker's voice.

"I'm sorry, what did you say?" asked Mrs. Villarreal as her thoughts were brought back to the present.

"I wondered if you wished to name the child. We must have a name to be able to admit him and start his medical history."

Without a moment's pause she answered, "Emilio... Emilio Villarreal." And with that she leaned over the tiny boy and kissed him lightly on the forehead. Crystal reluctantly handed the baby into the social workers arms, and then wiped her face with the inside of her elbow. She too kissed the defenseless child and together the two women walked solemnly out of the hospital and out of Emilio's life.

Emilio stayed in the hospital for three days as the medical staff tended to his basic needs. When the doctors assessed that Emilio was ready to be released from the hospital, the Saint Vincent de Paul orphanage was called to retrieve the little boy.

Emilio spent almost 10 months at the orphanage before I received the phone call that would cause our life stories to cross. The pediatrician at Saint Vincent de Paul had become increasingly alarmed at Emilio's lack of development. The orphanage was responsible for many abandoned and orphaned children, and it was difficult to give extra attention to any of them. So when there was a child who displayed any type of handicap or delay in his development, they would usually try to place the child in a smaller institution. Precious Miracles was the blessed institution to get the phone call for Emilio.

I went to pick Emilio up from the orphanage and was told of his severe special needs. I listened intently and scribbled down all the information about his past. Among the papers I was given was a medical diagnosis of cerebral palsy. Upon his arrival to our home, I made appointments with several specialists including a neurologist, a cardiologist, and a physical therapist. After meeting separately with all of them, we discovered that Emilio had been misdiagnosed. He did not have cerebral palsy. What he did have was chronic hemiplegia, which is paralysis of one side of the body. His brain was not at all affected, and his condition only required some extensive physical therapy.

Shortly after Emilio's arrival, we were blessed to be given free hippotherapy. This therapy uses horses for rehabilitation purposes. I have to admit, I was extremely skeptical about the results. It was offered to our foundation for free, and I was willing to give it a try since I figured I had nothing to lose. So, once a week for the next two years I took three, four or five of our special needs children to ride the horses at a nearby stable. I must sheepishly admit that every single one of our children improved with the hippotherapy. The children with spasticity, loosened up and became more flexible.

Children with no sense of balance were given the gift of equilibrium, and children who were told they would never walk, walked. Of all the children however, Emilio's improvement was the most exceptional. He exceeded everyone's expectations. He learned to walk, climb stairs, feed himself and basically do all the tasks of a healthy child of his same age.

Praise the Lord! Praise O servants of the Lord, Praise the name of the Lord! Blessed be the name of the Lord from this time forth and forevermore! From the rising of the sun to its going down the Lord's name is to be praised (Psalm 113: 1-8).

The Lord is high above all the nations, His glory above the heavens, Who is like the Lord our God, who dwells on high? Who humbles Himself to behold the things that are in the heavens and in the earth? He raises the poor out of the dust, and lifts the needy out of the ash heap, That He may seat him with princes, with the princes of His people.

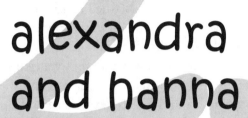

23

alexandra and hanna

Secret Babies

Elaine lived with her husband and four boys in Lago Agrio, Ecuador. Her husband worked on the oil pipelines and would sometimes be gone for weeks at a time. On one of his frequent trips, Elaine had an affair with her neighbor. Now she was certain there was a child growing inside her. She felt panicked. Her husband would know the child was not his, since he had been gone for so long. How would she tell him what she had done? Would he leave her? Would he try to take her boys from her? In a moment of loneliness had she ruined her entire life?

She mechanically started to straighten up her house, fretting over how she would solve her dilemma. As she, did she came across a small piece of ripped notebook paper with a number on it. It was the phone number of her husband's sister, Isabel who lived in Quito. She picked up her phone and dialed the number. When she heard the familiar voice she said, "Isabel it's me, Elaine. I'm in a big mess, and I wondered if there was something you could do to help me. But you must not tell your brother." Elaine then proceeded to explain her predicament to Isabel.

After hearing her story, Isabel said, "So you want me to ask my boss if she'll take your baby?"

"What? Who's your boss? Why would your boss take my baby? What are you talking about?"

"I work for a home for abandoned children called Precious Miracles. Isn't that why you called me?"

"Uh… no," started Elaine. "I had no idea where you worked. I didn't even know you had a job. Your boss takes in babies who are abandoned?" she clarified.

"Yes. I have been working for over two years with her. She's a foreigner who started a foundation and she takes in orphans. My coworkers and I help her take care of the babies until they get adopted. Then more babies come in, and then they get adopted. And so on."

Elaine almost dropped the phone. "Well, yes then. I guess that would work. I'll tell everyone I'm going to Quito to work. I'll give birth there, leave the baby with your boss and then come back. No one has to know."

Elaine followed through with her plan. She lied to her mother, saying she had been offered a job in Quito. She asked her mother to please look after her grandsons. Then she met up with her sister in law. Meanwhile, Isabel told me of the situation, and I agreed to take in the baby when he or she was born.

Some people have asked if it was hard to turn children away. The amazing thing about God's sovereignty is that it is perfect. God already knew how hard it would be for me to refuse a needy child. And so He ordered things in such a way where I would not have to turn children away. It was perfectly prepared how the children entered and exited our home. Our beds remained perpetually full. When a child would return to his birth mother or go in adoption, I would get a phone call usually within a few weeks requesting the placement of a child. When the rooms were full, the phone inexplicably stopped ringing with requests to take in children. It was perfectly structured and therefore from God.

As Elaine's due date came near however, I had fourteen children at home. I had tried for a long time to keep the maximum capacity to 10. Then I had increased that number to 12. Now we had 14 and one on the way. I had total peace that Elaine's baby was to be part of our family and so although it did not make sense, I agreed to receive her. One week before Elaine delivered, we were gifted with a brand new bassinet. I knew it was for my new baby.

When the baby was born, I was immediately notified. It was late, and I knew the hospital would not allow visitors, so I waited for the next day. Then I went to visit the baby girl. I asked Elaine if she wished to name her daughter. "No," she answered. "This is hard enough as it is."

"Well then her name is Alexandra," I stated. "After my sister."

Alexandra was a perfectly healthy baby girl. Elaine tearfully handed her child over to me, shaking her head as she repeated, "There's just no other way." She kissed the top of her daughter's head and crossed her forehead with thumb saying, "God bless you my baby."

When Elaine had lost most of the pregnancy weight, she went back to Lago Agrio to her family. Once at home, she discovered that her husband had left her for another woman.

She was devastated, but she knew that she couldn't fight or judge him. She too had been unfaithful. Her only reason for giving up Alexandra was now gone, so she returned to Precious Miracles to see if she could have her daughter back.

I was delighted that she had changed her mind, although not delighted with the circumstances. A couple of months had already passed, which implied the abandonment papers had to be undone. It required quite a bit of red tape, but before too long, Alexandra belonged legally once again to her birth mother. Two other children had also left by then, and just like clockwork, Precious Miracles was back down to the much more manageable number of 12.

Elaine and Alexandra visited us a few times in the coming years and the mother- daughter bond was undeniable. I am certain that God orchestrated Isabel's employment with me to provide a home for Alexandra when she needed one.

Lindsey was also expecting a child she had not planned on having. She was sixteen years old and had never been around babies. What would she do with one of her own? Her boyfriend had found out he had impregnated her and disappeared. She knew she couldn't count on him for support. Her thoughts whirled around in her head as she tried to think of what she would do. Her parents would surely be livid when they found out she was pregnant. Would they disown her? Would they kick her out of their home? Would they never speak to her again? Suddenly, she remembered that a few weeks ago they had suggested she get a job in the capital as a live-in maid. Her older cousins had recommended her for a job with a middle-aged couple whose children were grown and living with their respective families.

Lindsey's belly was not showing yet, and she knew she would be able to put off telling her parents her embarrassing secret.

She brought up the subject of working in Quito to her mother who thought it was a great idea. She would benefit from learning some responsibility in her life, and one less mouth to feed was going to make things a bit easier on the family's already tight financial circumstances.

Lindsey settled in easily at her new house. She was a quick learner and she picked up her housekeeping duties with ease. She would follow all her employer's directions throughout the day and then retire to her quiet, lonely bedroom in the back of the house at night to watch TV. Many nights she cried as she rubbed her hand across her stomach. It wasn't long before her pregnancy was apparent, and she was unable to put off telling her employers her false pretense for coming to work for them. Barbara, her employer, brought her into the living room one day.

"Sit down," she said, patting the maroon colored suede couch beside her. "I can see that you're expecting a child. Is that why you came to work for us? Are you hiding your pregnancy from your parents? What do you plan on doing when your baby arrives?" she asked.

"I don't know," stammered Lindsey, looking down at the floor.

"Do your parents know you're pregnant?"

"No, that's why I came here; to hide until I'm ready to tell them. But I don't know if I'll ever be ready. I think my dad may kill me. I don't know how to take care of a baby. I don't know if I can work here and take care of my baby."

"My best friend, Ines, goes to a Bible study with a lady who runs a home for unwanted children. Do you want to talk to her?"

"My baby isn't unwanted," cried Lindsey. "I do want my child. I just can't!"

"I know, dear. But maybe this woman can take your baby to avoid any more complications. Let's ask Ines to talk to her and see what we can do."

Lindsey cried herself to sleep that night, but the next morning she agreed that giving up her baby was the only alternative.

At our next Monday night Bible study, Ines approached me with the predicament. I told her I would be happy to reserve a place at Precious Miracles for Lindsey's baby. I began making the necessary arrangements for our new arrival. As the time for Lindsey's due date came closer, I felt myself getting more and more excited. My heart would flutter every time the phone rang as I waited for the call from the hospital. The day finally arrived. I received the call that Lindsey was in labor. I went to the hospital to pick up the much awaited child.

Lindsey was very sick, and had to stay in the hospital. She had a high fever for over a week, which obstructed our plan of taking baby Hanna immediately. The hospital could not release Lindsey, and they never release a newborn baby without the mother.

After almost two weeks, Lindsey had recovered and she was released. I drove to the hospital to pick up little Hanna. Lindsey had been nursing her baby for two weeks and they already had an unquestionable bond. The fear of her parents convinced her to go through with the plan of giving me her child.

After fully recovering, Lindsey returned home to her parents. One afternoon in a casual conversation, she asked her parents hypothetically what would happen if she had a baby.

They looked at each other and then her dad said, "We'd be disappointed, but we will always love you and we would help you raise your baby."

Lindsey couldn't believe what she was hearing. She had never in a million years expected that answer. With tears splattering on her cheeks she said, "I gave birth to a daughter. She is in Quito at a home for children."

Without a second thought, they were packing overnight bags to come to Quito to pick up baby Hanna. The process of returning Hanna was relatively simple, since not very much time had passed. In fact, Lindsey was still able to nurse her daughter.

I'll never know this side of heaven why God allowed me so much time with some of the children and so little time with others. But I am convinced that He had a perfect plan for each of the children to have been brought to our doors. Seeing 16-year old Lindsey walk out the door of our home with her tiny infant was difficult for me. I had the prideful thought that I could do a better job at caring for Hanna then the inexperienced girl that would be taking over for me. But I was reminded that I needed to trust God with every one of the precious miracles. He was in charge of the ones that remained in my home and under my custody, as well as all the little ones I had released. God is always in control.

24

laurie
A Tragic Beginning

Laurie stood with one foot on the side-walk and the other on the asphalt. The sky was overcast, and her little body shook from the combination of cold air and nervousness she felt.

"Go!" yelled her mother, shoving her three-year old daughter into the street. "Your uncle is right over there," she said, holding out a finger pointed to the other side of the street to a little store front.

Laurie ran across the street as commanded. Just as she reached the other side, she heard a car zoom behind her. She approached her uncle who was sitting precariously on a rickety wooden stool. Her shaky hand pulled a small plastic bag wrapped in toilet tissue out from between her stomach and the elastic waist line in her dirty, blue sweatpants. Her mother had told her to give it to her uncle.

"Be discreet!" he screamed at her, grabbing at the packet and looking nervously from side to side. Laurie didn't say a word. She had repeated this routine many times before.

But this time would be different. Two men in identical brown uniforms came around the corner. Laurie's uncle pushed her to the ground as a distraction and took off running down the street. Laurie picked herself up off the ground and looked across the street to find her mother. There was no one there.

The men who were police officers knelt down beside her.

"What's your name little one?" asked the taller of the two.

Laurie didn't say a word and didn't make eye contact.

"You're right Steve," he said to his partner. "They are using the little girl as a drug mule.

She is the vessel that transports the cocaine from one dealer to the other. I didn't believe it until I saw it with my own eyes. We can't allow them to continue. What do we do with her?"

As he was still speaking, a fourteen-year old boy poked his head out of a window of the store. "Please don't take my cousin," he cried. "She is so little. This is the only life she knows."

The two officers questioned William, the cousin, and got more details about the situation. Members of Laurie's entire family were drug traffickers. Many times they used her as a scapegoat or as the mule. William had his share of being the mule as well. He loved his little cousin and was afraid he would never see her again. The police decided to take them both to a rehab center to get them out of danger. As more and more details became known, the officers realized that this family was notorious all over the south of Quito for their drug mafia. They were sneaky and good at their job. They had managed to escape the police and prison, time and time again. Laurie and her siblings had been surrounded by, and directly exposed to illegal drugs for their entire lives. William and Laurie spent that night in the rehab center.

The next day, I received a phone call informing me of a little girl who needed a home.

Precious Miracles' policy was to take in children from newborn to age two. My reasoning behind this policy was that older children had a set of different troubles. Our house was designed for small children, and this was apparent as one saw the toys, and the sizes of our clothes. Older children would bring to our home more mental trauma and behavior issues that babies would not.

I cannot explain exactly why I chose to say yes to Laurie that day. As I was listening to the case on the phone, I saw little Elsie with no one of her same age to play with. I also fast forwarded my imagination to see what type of life Laurie would live. I knew this precious child would live a life of utter torture if I did not open my doors to her. And last, but certainly not least, I felt an overwhelming sense of peace that God had a purpose in me receiving this phone call.

I jotted down the address for the rehab center and told them I would be there in the morning. I had retrieved children by myself many times before, but for some reason this time I decided not to go alone. I called my mom, who graciously agreed to accompany me. Because the address was vague, I parked my car at a hotel and we took a taxi.

God was in every one of these steps. As we would soon discover, the location of the rehab center was in a very horrible part of town. I am so thankful that I chose not to go alone and not to drive my car to such a frightening area. Our taxi driver got very lost, and my mom was sure that he was going to give up and get us all out of the slums. He was persistent and we finally arrived. We paid him and asked him to please wait for us as we would need a ride out of there.

The 'Home of Life' center was surrounded by 12 foot cement walls. Curly masses of barbed wire and broken glass lined the top of the walls. A giant black metal gate was the entrance.

"It looks like a jail!" I said to my mom.

We knocked on the gate, and as the pounding echoed back to me, I felt like I was in medieval times knocking on the gate of dungeon. I half expected an ogre to open it. A little slat opened up and we gave our names and our reason for being there.

We were ushered quickly inside and greeted by two social workers who proceeded to explain the rehab center's policy. They only housed adults. There was no room for children here and it frankly was not a safe place for a child. Since Laurie was three years old, she could not stay. They went on to tell us a little of Laurie's past. They mentioned the likeliness of her being physically and possibly sexually abused. My stomach was in knots as I thought, "What have I agreed to? What if it is too late for this little girl? What if too much damage has already been done to her? What if I can't help her?"

I reviewed the legal forms I had been handed and signed on several dotted lines, as we waited for them to bring us Laurie. When the employee of the center walked in with a child in her arms, I was confused. Who was this little boy? Surely there was some mistake.

"Laurie," she said affectionately, "These nice ladies are going to take you to a nice place."

I caught my breath as I realized that this homely little boy was not a boy, it was the sweet little girl I had come to rescue. I reached out my hand to her and said, "It's nice to meet you. I'm Stacey and this is my mom Sharon. My children are at home and they need someone to play with. Would you like to come with me to see our toys and to play with my children?" She nodded silently and slowly.

I held out my arms and she willingly entered them. As directed by the social workers, we had to sneak her out so that her cousin would not see us. They reiterated how dangerous her family was and that if they knew we had her, we would be placing our lives in imminent danger. When we exited the big black gate, I was truly astounded that our taxi was still waiting for us. He drove us back to our car, commenting on how dangerous that area of town was.

Laurie was completely silent the whole way home. When we arrived, she looked scared and confused. I introduced her to the other children who were jumping up and down with excitement.

I took Laurie in to the kitchen with me to help me start on dinner. I asked her to put a bib on every high chair and at each place setting, while I filled a pot with water for the macaroni. She was quiet and her face looked sad. I knelt down beside her and said, "No one is ever going to hurt you here. I know this is scary and you don't know where you are, but I am going to be your mommy and you are going to live here with us." She nodded.

"We have lots of food here and you won't be hungry," I said, showing her our abundantly stocked pantry. She nodded again without saying a word. We continued to get dinner ready and when it was done, I turned the stove off and took her back to the bedrooms. We went in to the room Elsie and Edna slept in, and I set up a little toddler bed for her. She helped me put the Winnie the Pooh sheets on it and then chose a bright pink Hawaiian flower quilt to go on top. "Good choice!" I said.

I opened the closet to show her the dresses. "All these pretty clothes are for you to share with Elsie." She again nodded silently. "We have oodles of fun toys. Do you think you will like living here?" She nodded once more, but did not say a word. In fact, the only thing Laurie said that whole afternoon and evening to me was that she needed to use the bathroom. I was thrilled that she was potty trained, but alarmed that she did not speak at all.

She ate dinner quietly. I gave her a bath and she just looked down into the water the whole time. My heart was pounding. "Lord what do I do to reach her?" I asked. "How can I let her know that she is safe and that she is loved?"

Every night at Precious Miracles we had devotions after all the children were bathed.

We sat in the living room and after telling them a story from our Toddler Bible, we all took turns praying. That night as we made our way around the circle, I asked Laurie if she wanted to pray. She shook her head silently.

I somewhat expected her first night to be a difficult one because she was so frightened.

Much to my surprise and delight she was asleep within minutes of lying down.

The next day she warmed up a little more. I included her in preschool time and she played and interacted with the other children. We made crepe paper flowers and I was happy to see her participate. Then we played a game where we went around the house looking for things with flowers on them. While most of the children ran outside to pick dandelions, Laurie quickly ran to her bed and grabbed her quilt. I was thrilled to discover how bright she was.

After dinner, I took her back to the bedroom to give her a bath. I bathed her and then scooped her out of the tub and wrapped her towel around her. As I was putting her pajamas on, I tickled her tummy and she giggled. "Praise God! She giggles!" I said out loud. Then I said, "I love you Laurie. Do you know that? Do you know who I am?"

She smiled big and said, "You are my Mommy." Other than asking to use the bathroom, it was the first phrase out of her mouth.

My heart skipped and my eyes flooded with tears as I said, "I sure am sweet little girl. I sure am."

How can one explain that after just one day a child could be that secure and comfortable? After all the trauma and pain she had experienced and seen in her little life, she was ready to trust again. She had embraced me as her mother and she was ready to move forward with her life. I used to dwell on how much I had been hurt by other people in my past and how difficult it was to trust again. My precious little Laurie taught me so much about forgiveness.

That night as we made the rounds at prayer time, I asked Laurie if she wished to pray.

She nodded. She clasped her little hands together and bowed her head. Her little mutterings were too quiet and muffled for me to understand, but I know God heard them.

The next day we had our regularly scheduled appointment with our beautician. I had been fortunate enough to find a professional beautician who was a Christian and who offered to come every month to cut all the children's hair for free. Laurie had only been in our house for three days, and I thought it was probably too soon for her to get her hair cut. Her hair was thin and sparse as a result of her extreme malnutrition. I thought she had experienced enough newness in the first days that we didn't have to add any more confusion to her adaptation.

But as all the other children waited their turn to sit on the stool to get fixed up, I saw Laurie in the doorway watching. I went over to her and asked if she would like to get her hair cut. She smiled and nodded. So we sat her down, put the plastic cape over her neck, and the beautician proceeded to even out her fine curls. As she sat there, I offered her a hand-held mirror. She looked into it and made a funny face, then gasped at her reflection.

My mom who was also there, noticed. "Stacey, I don't think she's ever seen her reflection!" she said.

We both turned to observe Laurie and smiled to see my mom's hypothesis was true.

The way she reacted to her reflection made it clear to both of us that she had never seen her image in a mirror before. It was comical to see her stick out her tongue and then jump back at the image with the outstretched tongue in front of her. Long after the stylist was done with Laurie's new hairstyle, Laurie was still holding the mirror in front of her. She was completely mesmerized by the novel toy.

As I see the beautiful little girl that Laurie has become, I am stunned at how she arrived.

The day I met her I actually thought she was a little boy. She had rather prominent ears, and a droopy eye lid. She was bony with a gaunt face. She was almost bald. Now Laurie is a remarkably beautiful child. Her smile lights up any room and her princess complex is hard to ignore. If there is anything sparkly or glittery she wants it. She chooses to wear only dresses, and if they are pink, that is even better. She loves jewelry and play make-up, and she insists on having her hair done every day.

In 1844 Hans Christian Anderson wrote a story that has become famous over the years. Here is an excerpt.

But what did she see in the clear stream below? Her own image; no longer a dark, gray bird, ugly and disagreeable to look at, but a graceful and beautiful swan. She now felt glad at having suffered sorrow and trouble, because it enabled her to enjoy so much better all the pleasure and happiness around her; for the great swans swam round the new-comer, and stroked her neck with their beaks, as a welcome.

Into the garden presently came some little children, and threw bread and cake into the water.

"See," cried the youngest, "there is a new one;" and the rest were delighted, and ran to their father and mother, dancing and clapping their hands, and shouting joyously, "There is another swan come; a new one has arrived."

Then they threw more bread and cake into the water, and said, "The new one is the most beautiful of all; she is so young and pretty." And the old swans bowed their heads before her.

She had been persecuted and despised for her ugliness, and now she heard them say she was the most beautiful of all the birds. Even the elder-tree bent down its bows into the water before her, and the sun shone warm and bright. Then she rustled her feathers, curved her slender neck, and cried joyfully, from the depths of her heart, "I never dreamed of such happiness as this, while I was an ugly duckling."

Laurie's first weeks with us were not without trials. It took extensive time and effort to undo the harm that had been such a normal part of her existence. One day she woke up from her nap, and she had wet herself in her sleep. She stood in the corner of the play room with a panicked look on her face and her whole body was trembling. When I realized that she was wet, I held out my hand to walk her back to the bedroom. "Let's get you changed," I said. She screamed and cried and refused to go with me. It took a lot of patient insisting to assure her that I was not angry with her and that I knew it was just an accident.

Laurie also refused to leave the house. She did not even want to go with all the other children up the street to a public park. She hated being outside. I think the memory of her life out on the streets was too fresh in her mind. She would prefer to stay in the house with a puzzle by herself than to join the rest of the children in the yard.

She threw tantrums if I put her in the car to go somewhere. I rationalized that she was probably afraid that if she got in my car, I was going to take her back to her family.

Laurie was also a very sick little girl, and it took quite a few rounds of parasite medicine to eliminate the worms that had invaded her body.

Two months after Laurie's arrival was Christmas. She was almost four years old but she had never celebrated Christmas. In fact, she had never even received a gift in her life.

She observed wide-eyed as I handed out presents to the other children. Then I found a gift under the tree for her. I dramatically read the card on the top of the pretty package, "to Laurie from Mommy Stacey." She had a smile from ear to ear! She was overwhelmed with delight as I handed her the gift. She received it from me and gripped it in her little fingers. She was sitting on my dad's lap, and he pointed out to me that she was not opening her gift.

I sat down on the floor beside her and said, "Tear the paper Sweetie. It's better inside!"

She didn't want to tear the pretty red and green paper, so I helped her carefully open the sides with the tape. We took our time and opened the paper gently so as not to rip it.

The other children sat around the tree patiently waiting. They had all experienced Christmas before and fully understood the routine, but they were very sweet to wait for their sister to catch on.

When the package was finally opened, she saw a doll inside. She gasped and squeezed the doll to her chest. We had a toy box full of dolls in one corner of the play room that she had seen since the day she arrived. We had no shortage of dolls or other toys. But Laurie knew that this doll was extra special because it was hers. It was the very first thing anyone had ever set aside specifically for her.

Laurie received several other gifts that morning and among them was a pair of pink butterfly shoes. She carried the doll and the shoes around for the next three days. They came into the dining area with her at every meal, and she brought them into bed with her every night.

Just a few months after Christmas, it was the date of Carla's fourth birthday. She, of course, had never had a birthday party either, and we made sure it was special. We decorated the house in a Disney princess theme and her gifts were all girly girl gifts. My little swan was happy.

Several months passed and Laurie was increasingly more comfortable in our home with our customs and routines. Then one day the door bell rang. I went outside to answer it, and waiting for me was a man with a motorcycle. When I approached him he handed me a paper. "You've been served." He stated.

"What?" I asked. I looked at the paper in my hands and then looked up and he was already driving off down the street. I opened up the paper and read the words that I was to appear the next day at 10:00 a.m. at a courthouse. Under reason it simply stated: regarding Laurie Moreno.

I called my dad to let him know and he offered to go with me. The next day I got Laurie dressed up and packed a little backpack with a coloring book, some crayons and her doll. My dad drove us to the address on the paper. I announced our arrival and was acknowledged by a large overweight woman with gray hair. "Wait out there!" she shouted, pointing her finger past me and refusing to look up.

I raised my eyebrows at my dad and complied. I sat with Laurie and my dad for 20 minutes in the small waiting area. I tried to keep Laurie entertained. When they were ready for us, we were called in to the office. The three of us walked in and took our seats.

"Who are you?" shouted the woman again.

"My name is Stacey Smith. I am the Director of the Precious Miracles Foundation," I said, making a point to use a quiet voice in an effort to hint that I was not hard of hearing and did not require shouting. "This is Laurie Moreno, the girl in question and this is my father who has accompanied me this morning."

The woman turned to the three other people in the room and rolled her eyes. "What is the situation?" she asked.

"Well, honestly I am not sure." I answered. "I received this notice yesterday at my home and I am obeying orders." With that, I stood to hand her the paper.

"SIT DOWN!" she yelled.

I did so with my mouth gaping open.

"So you're the one that stole this child from her family?" she asked.

"I'm sorry, what did you say?" I asked incredulously.

"You stole this child from the Home of Life," she repeated. "This child has a family and you stole her from them. What is your intent? Do you plan on smuggling her out to someone in your country? Why did you steal the child?"

"You are mistaken," I said shortly. "I have not stolen this or any other child. I was asked by the Home of Life to take in an abandoned child and I agreed. She was being used by her parents as a drug mule and the police removed her from her family. The police took her to the Home of Life, who in turn called me because they are not set up to care for young children."

"And what gives you the right to take in abandoned children?" she asked. "You think because you are an American you can come solve all our third world problems?"

"I have legal permission to operate as a home for abandoned children in this country." I said defensively.

"Nonsense!" she screamed. "How come I have never heard of this Precious Miracles you speak of?"

"I'm not sure..." I started "Wait outside!" she screamed again.

I picked up little Laurie in my arms and walked out the door. I was shaking from head to food. I turned to my dad and asked, "Did that just happen? Did I just get screamed at, accused of kidnapping?"

My dad was silently shaking his head from side to side. He sighed deeply. We waited for almost two hours. I had not anticipated spending that much time, and I was trying to think creatively of ways to occupy my little four-year old.

When they finally came out of the meeting room, the hateful woman looked at us.

"You're still here?" she asked.

"You asked me to wait." I reminded her.

"You will be hearing from us," she threatened. "We are going to investigate this foundation of yours and see what you are attempting. What you are doing is not admissible. I will personally see to it that your foundation gets shut down." And with those words, she stormed out of the building.

I did not sleep for days after that encounter. Every time the doorbell rang, I rushed to the door to see if I was being subpoenaed again. When the phone rang my heart would sink. But I never heard from that woman again. My guess is that she did investigate and found us to be blameless in the eyes of the law. God had protected us once more.

25

john

The Miracle of Peace

I was finishing up the month's payroll when I answered my office phone at 3:00 that afternoon. A mere two and a half hours later, little 14-month old John was sitting in our play room, staring at the other children and all the brightly colored toys around him. I chuckled quietly as I thought of the question I heard so often, "What's a typical day like at Precious Miracles?" Typical most certainly did not exist in this house, but I wouldn't have it any other way. There was never a dull moment.

John's mother, Pamela, worked as a prostitute in a brothel in north Quito. She had made an arrangement to leave her baby boy in the care of an amiable neighbor family the nights she worked. The Tenorio family had been eager to watch John and was growing increasingly more attached to the little boy. Pamela would return after her night shifts and take her son back to their apartment. The following evening she would repeat the cycle. One morning, however, Pamela did not arrive to pick John up. The Tenorio family was happy to care for little John, thinking she would show up the next morning.

But two weeks went by and Pamela did not return. So Amie Tenorio called the authorities to see what she should do with the child.

"I'd be thrilled to keep him," she told the officer over the

211

phone. "He has become part of our family and I love him like my other children. I want to make sure everything is legal and I don't want to get into any trouble. I don't have any papers for the boy and I don't want to be accused of kidnapping." When asked for her address, she dictated it to the officer. Then the phone call was mysteriously over, and Amie had more questions than when she had started. Before she could plan her next step, police were at her home.

They began to pry little John out of Amie's arms as she protested. "No! This is not what I wanted to happen. I told you, I'll keep him. I just wanted you to tell me how to keep him legally…" Her voice trailed off as she could see the officers were not going to change their minds. They wriggled the crying baby free from her tight grip and placed him in the back seat of their patrol car. Amie watched powerlessly, as the officers drove away.

Within a few minutes the police car pulled up to an orphanage. One officer got out of the vehicle with John, rang the doorbell and dropped him haphazardly in the arms of the mother superior, Sister Josephine. She looked down at the wailing child in her arms and shouted at the officers as they drove off, "This child is too young! Stop!" But once again the officers were not going to change their minds. Sister Josephine's institution was a home for boys ages 5-18. John was just over a year old. There was nothing she could do at that moment, the officers had already left. The police seemed adamant about not allowing a child to be in the care of a loving family because of the lack of legal documents. It didn't seem to matter that he would be placed in an orphanage that was not structured for babies. By their logic, a legal orphanage was better than an illegal family.

It was evening when John and Sister Josephine had been brusquely introduced, and she took the baby back to where the other children were. She informed the other nuns that she would do all that she could to place this little boy in a better suited place, but for tonight, he would stay. John cried all night. When they tried to feed him, he refused. He did not want to be held and screamed if anyone came near him. His clothes were filthy, but the orphanage had no clothes his size to change him into.

The next morning, Sister Josephine was on the phone to several orphanages trying to find an appropriate placement for John. She called Melinda at For His Children and explained the situation. Melinda informed her that FHC had no vacant cribs and recommended she try calling Precious Miracles.

It was mid afternoon when I received the phone call from Sister Josephine. She told me of her predicament. She also warned me that John was having a very difficult time and had not stopped screaming and crying. I agreed to meet him. As I drove across town, I prayed. I prayed that God would give me peace about bringing John into my home. I prayed that John would stop his hysterical crying and that God would also give him peace about coming with me. When I walked into the office and greeted everyone there, I approached little John. I knelt down on the ground and said, "Hi handsome! I'm Stacey." John smiled and jumped into my arms with his chubby little arms wrapped around my neck. Everyone in the room, including Sister Josephine gasped.

"Well," I said. "I supposed this little one is a keeper! Where do I sign?" I was given the little information that was known about him, and all the while John never released his fixed grasp on my neck. I swallowed hard to stifle the tears. I thanked everyone and left with my new little boy.

Back at Precious Miracles, we bathed John and realized that had not been a very common occurrence for him, both by the amount of filth on his little body and the reaction he had. His little tummy was bloated severely out of proportion to the rest of his body. It was past our pediatrician's office hours, so we planned to have him examined the next day.

John ate his dinner with gusto and slept serenely all night on his clean sheets in his new crib. He did not cry once upon arriving to our home. God had answered my prayer. I had peace and John had peace.

Dr. Castillo knew me and my children well. He had seen all of them, treated all of them and been an enormous help to me. When we visited him the next day, he was alarmed.

"This child has third degree malnutrition," he stated. "He should be hospitalized to receive an IV." "Oh no!" I cried. "Doctor Castillo, this little boy has just had the most confusing and disruptive three days of his life. He has been passed around from a family to the police, to an orphanage and then to me. His entire schedule has been interrupted and everything he once knew has changed. But last night he did so well in my house. If he has to sleep in a new bed again tonight, around new people, I think it will seriously affect him." The words were rushing out of my mouth in my despair over the situation. I took a deep breath and said, "Is there any possible way I can treat him at home to prevent any more stress? Can you teach me how to put in an IV?"

Doctor Castillo smiled and sighed. "Only you would consider the child's emotional well- being as equally important as his physical well-being." He looked up at the ceiling quietly for a minute then continued, "We'll give him three days. I want you to feed him a very specific diet that I will write down for you. You will need to feed him six times a day.

Meanwhile, you will also need to give him the parasite elimination medicine him so that the parasites he evidently is carrying will not continue to eat all his nutrients. Come back in three days and if he needs to be hospitalized, you have to agree to do it."

"It's a deal!" I said with excitement. "If he's not better in three days, he's all yours! We both know, though, he will be better." I winked as I scooped up my little baby and walked out of the office.

I stopped briefly at the pharmacy to pick up the necessary parasite medication and then hurried home to begin my newest mission. For the next three days, I followed Dr. Castillo's orders strictly. I did not delegate his feedings or his medication to the staff, but instead took full responsibility for his portions and dosages. On the fourth morning, John and I returned to the clinic. Dr. Castillo examined John and smiled up at me. "If all my patients were like the little Miracles, I'd be out of a job," he joked. "You did it."

"No Doctor," I said. "God did it."

The next step in John's recovery was to have blood work done. Because of his mother's line of work, we needed to rule out any sexually transmitted diseases that could have been passed on to him at birth. Dr. Castillo had filled out the order form for the blood tests. He had checked all the STD boxes and had also written the phrase, "Mother is a prostitute" under the box marked 'Reason For Tests'. I took John into the lab to get the blood taken. The nurse took my paper and looked up at me with a questioning and disgusting look on her face. It took me a few seconds to realize that she assumed I was the mother of the child.

"Oh!" I said impulsively. "I'm not the prostitute! I just care for the child."

She laughed nervously and we proceeded with the blood tests. The tests were back in three days, and I was ecstatic to find out that John did not have any disease.

We continued to keep a close watch on John's diet, and his health progressively improved. Within a month of his arrival, he was walking. He was 15 months old, but he had been unable to balance his body weight because of his skinny legs and large tummy. With his body in better proportion, he was up and moving all over our house.

As we proceeded with John's health, we also proceeded with his legal status of abandonment. We were able to contact Amie, and she came to visit John on a few occasions. She mentioned how she had been willing to adopt him, but she was not sure if she would be able to do so financially. She had four children of her own and it was difficult to make ends meet. I assured her that if we were unable to return him to his birth mother that we would find him a good home. I asked her to give me any information that she had on Pamela. Amie said she hadn't seen Pamela since the last day that John had been dropped off at her house.

A few weeks later, however, Amie called, telling me that Pamela had returned. So along with my social worker, Ximena, we went to north Quito to locate her. We were able to find her and she was willing to talk to us. My heart was warmed as I noticed the incredible physical resemblance she had with her son. We talked for a long while with Pamela and asked repeatedly if she wanted us to return her son to her. She cried freely in our presence explaining her own story. She had been abandoned at birth and was taken in by a family who ended up treating her more like a slave than part of the family.

She was physically, verbally and sexually abused during her entire childhood and adolescence. At age 16, she finally got up the nerve to leave the abusive cycle and ran away. Unfortunately, she had no birth certificate or any other type of document that proved her existence. She had also never set foot inside of a classroom and was completely illiterate. She had felt her only option for survival was selling her body. She had been a prostitute for ten years.

She also confessed that she did not wish for John to grow up knowing his mother was a hooker. She had gotten pregnant by one of her clients, but had no idea which one. She was afraid to tell John one day that she did not know who his father was. She mentioned that when he was a baby, it didn't seem to matter what she did. But as he grew older, there would be no way to hide the harsh reality from him.

I offered Pamela a job at Precious Miracles, or help finding a different job. I also told her that I could try to find a place for her to live so that she could leave the lifestyle she was so wrapped up in. Ximena chimed in, assuring Pamela that she still had options and that she should not feel like she had to continue with this lifestyle forever. Pamela looked down at the floor, shaking her head. "I don't know," she said repeatedly.

Ximena seized the moment to witness to Pamela. She assured her that it was never too late to turn to God. She told her of the plan of salvation and that it was for everyone.

Pamela never took her eyes off of Ximena as she listened intently to her words. She was told about grace and how none of us deserve to go to heaven, but we have the gift of eternal life through Jesus Christ's death on the cross. After several minutes of silence, Ximena asked Pamela if she wished to accept Jesus into her life. Pamela nodded.

Ximena asked me to pray, and I did so emotionally. Pamela repeated after me that she knew she was a sinner and that nothing she could ever do on her own could grant her entry into heaven. She then accepted that Jesus Christ was the Son of God and had died on the cross for her sins. And finally she repeated that she wanted her life to change, and she wanted Jesus to be the Lord and Savior of her life.

After the prayer, we all hugged and cried. I gave Pamela directions to Precious Miracles and invited her to come and visit anytime she wished. I also told her that if she ever thought she could take care of John again that we would eagerly return him to her.

Pamela only came to our home once after that, and then I never heard from her again.

Only God knows what really took place in her heart that afternoon.

John continued to grow and thrive in his temporary home with us. He quickly became everyone's favorite in spite of our best intentions to be fair. His adoption paperwork seemed to take forever, but it was all part of God's perfect timing in preparing his forever family. John's adaptation with his mother and father was one of the quickest we had ever experienced. When it was time for him to leave, he did so willingly and excitedly. John's story with us started out tragically and ended fantastically.

26

alison
My Precious Daughter

While attempting to feed Jacque her bottle and simultaneously check my e-mail, my phone rang. I smiled down at the alert little baby in my arms and said, "This is called multi-tasking, sweetheart." I reached over to pick up the receiver as a thought flew into my head. How many times had I picked up this very phone and had my life completely changed? I wondered if it was about to happen again.

I scribbled down the facts as quickly as my pen would allow. "She's two years old?" I clarified out loud. "Hydrocephalus," I repeated as I wrote down the word. "Sure, we would love to take her. That's what we're here for. Okay then, I'll be at the Baca Ortiz hospital tomorrow at 3:00, taking a child to physical therapy. Can you meet me there?"

I hung up the phone and instinctively lifted Jacque over my shoulder and patted her back. I read through the notes I had just made. I remembered hydrocephalus meant water on the brain. I had taken care of a little baby with hydrocephalus when I worked at the Crisis Nursery in Arizona. He had received a shunt and he was a completely healthy child. No big deal, I thought to myself. We will have a shunt put in this little girl's head and she'll be fine. I called my mom to see if she could give me a hand the next day with Sebastian's physical therapy and receiving another miracle. I never had to do much convincing where meeting and picking up children was involved. She was elated.

The next day, I put together a diaper bag for a two-year old child. I tossed in some large diapers, an outfit, a package of crackers, and a tub of wet wipes. I strapped a toddler car seat in and told Sebastian to get in beside it.

"Tia Stacey, who is going with us?" he asked.

"Oh, no one is buddy. We're going to meet a little girl at your hospital visit," I explained.

"We may bring her home with us. That's why there's a car seat. Now buckle up. We're going to pick up Abuela first, Okay?"

"Hooray!" he shouted. "Abuela's coming!"

Sebastian's hydrotherapy appointment was at 2:00. I had told Hilda, the woman on the phone, 3:00 so that we could meet her on our way out. After drying Sebastian off and helping him redress, we went up the large stair case to the main entrance. My mom and I searched the enormous waiting area for a woman with a two-year old running around her. As we were still scouting out the place, a woman came toward us. She was carrying a large child in her arms, thoroughly wrapped up in a blanket.

"Miss Stacey?" she asked.

"Yes I am," I smiled. "Are you Hilda?"

She nodded. I introduced my mother, and Hilda introduced me to her friend who stood right behind her. "I can't hold her much longer," she panted. We made our way to some nearby chairs. She told me Alison's story as I looked into the smiling face in her arms.

"My elderly mother has been taking care of this child," she started. "She cannot lift her to bathe her or to even change her anymore. She has just gotten too big."

"Why does your mother have this child?" I questioned.

"Alison's mother, Nicole, is an orphan. My mother took Nicole in when she was a child.

Nicole had Alison when she was very young and left her with my mother. But there is something severely wrong with Alison. I haven't gone to see my mother in over a year," she continued looking, shamefully at the ground. "I went to visit her and was totally astonished when I saw Alison. My mother is 80. She cannot care for this child." And with that, she tried to sit Alison up in her arms and uncovered her blanket and hat.

I impulsively pulled back. I had never before seen a child as deformed as Alison. Her head was about four times larger than a child of her age would normally be. I shook my head vigorously. "Oh I'm so sorry," I started. "I had no idea. There is no way that Precious Miracles is equipped to handle a child with such severe special needs."

"Oh Miss Stacey," cried Hilda. "Don't say no. Please help us! You have to help us!"

I turned to my mom. "Mom!" I nearly yelled. "We can't! Look at her. I don't know the first thing about caring for a child like her." Despair shrouded my thoughts.

My mom's face was already wet with tears as she said, "If you don't take this little girl, Stacey, what will happen to her? You were called to the ones that no one else would care for. Look at that little girl. She really is the least of these, Honey. If you reject her as well, who will show her Christ's love?"

I turned back to Hilda and said, "Okay, we'll take Alison." People all around us were pointing and gawking. Some gasped and others snickered. Hilda and I talked for a few more minutes about her diet, medicines, etc.. I was surprised to find out that she really did not require more care than any other child. She drank from a bottle and she was used to lying on the floor all day long. She was on no medication. I gave Hilda all our contact information and told her to advise Alison's mother if she wanted to visit, we would be happy to receive her.

Hilda kissed Alison's forehead as she handed her to me. I was stunned at Alison's weight. We walked to the car, and it was immediately evident that she would not fit in the car seat. My mom sat in the back seat and held her, and Sebastian sat next to them. He had been silently taking in the whole series of events in the hospital waiting room. His eyes never left his new friend.

I drove home with extra caution that day. "How's she doing?" I called back to my mom, my eyes never leaving the road.

"Stacey, she hasn't stopped smiling! She is so sweet!"

Upon arriving back at Precious Miracles, I went in first to prepare the staff for our new family member. She had received enough staring and gasping for one day, and I did not want the employees to repeat my mistake. My mom helped me bathe her, and it was very apparent that she had not had a bath in an extremely long period of time. The stench that came off her dirty little body was nauseating.

Leaving Alison with my mom, I rummaged through our toddler clothes searching for tops that had buttons. She would not be able to wear any type of shirt or dress that went over the head. I found some zip-up pajamas and handed them to my mom. She finished dressing her as I proceeded to figure out Alison's sleeping arrangements.

All the cribs were on the second floor, and I could see that carrying her up and down stairs was not going to work well. With the help of one of the employees, we carried a crib down into my office. We speedily remodeled my office to include a comfortable space for Alison's bedroom.

The other children were pleasantly curious as they met their new sibling. Alison seemed to enjoy her new surroundings and playmates. From the time her face had been uncovered in the hospital, she had not stopped smiling. She was tremendously comfortable getting all the attention. I thought how easily frightened she could be in a new place surrounded by new people, sounds, and smells. She was not at all afraid though. As I sat on the floor holding her in my arms, a tear splashed off my cheek onto hers. "Oh Alison," I said to her. "How is it that you are so accepting of me when I was not accepting of you?" From that precise minute, my heart was softened. I knew that Alison had been divinely brought into my life and that God had a plan for joining us.

Alison had more medical concerns than what was initially revealed to me. Because of the hydrocephalus, her fontanels or soft spot had never closed, causing her skull to grow apart. Her oversized head was the result. It also meant that the top of her head was not protected by skull. Her skin was tightly stretched over the skull on the sides of her head and her brain was virtually unprotected. We had to take extra caution with her when we would carry, bathe, dress, or move her.

She also had spin bifida, which caused her to be paralyzed from the waist down. Potty training was out of the question, and she would never be able to crawl or walk. We had special chairs for her, and she did learn to be fairly independent. She loved to do arts and crafts, and her favorite thing was to have books read to her. She slept peacefully through the nights. She ate with an incredible appetite and eventually learned to feed herself. One of her highly preferred activities was music time. She would flap her arms to the rhythm of the music as her siblings would dance around her.

After very little time with Alison, I knew she was my daughter. All the children that could speak called me Mommy, and I loved every child deeply. But the love I felt for Alison was a distinct, more intense love. She undeniably was my little girl.

Shortly after coming to this conclusion, I went to an orphanage directors meeting. There, the guest speaker was a lawyer who was explaining the changes in the adoption laws.

He explained that until a child's adoption certificate was signed, the birth parents always maintained legal rights to their child, even if they had abandoned that child or had not been actively caring for the child. My heart sunk when I heard this. Right then and there, I knew I needed to legally adopt Alison. I could not bear the thought of her ever leaving me or belonging to someone else. That very day when the meeting was adjourned, I approached the lawyer and asked for specifics on adopting a child with special needs.

In the next week, the process to become Alison's permanent mommy had been started.

Raising a child with many medical problems and extreme special needs did not worry or frighten me. I felt as if Alison had been born to me, and it was never an option for me not to be her mother. I had learned how to best care for her and had revolved my life around her. I had provided her with her own unique wardrobe and had made necessary adjustments around the house to accommodate her needs.

Every morning she joined me in the kitchen while I prepared breakfast for the other children. Many times she would sit in the office with me, coloring her books while I finished financial reports, staff schedules, or my Bible Institute homework. She went with me every week to church. I had special routines with her such as reading her stories before bed and tucking her in myself. We prayed every night before she went to sleep. In many ways, although the legal certificate was not completed, she was already my daughter.

My biggest struggle was never with Alison's care, but rather others' opinions of her. It was so difficult to take her out in public and to withstand the incessant gawking. People seemed to be shameless as they would point and stare. Others would come up to me and gasp, "what is wrong with your child?" This became such a normal part of our outings that I had come to expect it. One day, in the waiting room of the doctor's office, a little girl approached me. She couldn't have been more than six years old. Here it comes, I thought, as I braced myself for the curious questions that would follow.

"Is she your baby?" asked the little girl.

"Yes she is." I answered taking a deep breath.

"She is so beautiful. She looks just like you," she said.

My heart skipped as I looked into the eyes of this darling child in front of me. Somehow this little girl could see past Alison's unpleasant deformity to see the truly beautiful child that she was. I found it adorable that she could think that Alison looked like me, since there was no physical way that was possible.

"Thank you," I choked. "Thank you very much." I turned my gaze toward Alison and said, "Did you hear that princess? She said you're beautiful!"

Alison smiled up at me. The nurse called the little girl's name and she said, "Oh I have to go now! Goodbye Precious!"

Ali waved her little hand and smiled at her new friend.

I ran into the intensive care unit to see how my baby was doing. Why hadn't they called me? I had left last night at the doctor's urging, knowing things were not looking good. But they said they'd call to let me know how she was doing and they hadn't. Did that mean she was doing better? What was going on? I headed toward the nurse's station to ask for information. An older doctor was there, speaking on the phone.

"Things are not well with the Bedoya child," I heard him say. I stopped abruptly to eavesdrop more. He did not notice me and would never have known that I was the mother of the

Bedoya child. "She has had two more heart attacks this morning. She is on life support now. I do not think there is hope for this little girl."

I felt like I was spinning, and I grabbed a hold of the counter to steady myself. The doctor noticed my reaction to his words and got off the phone. He turned to look at me. His eyes told me he realized he had just made the mistake of allowing a mother to hear news she never wants to hear. "Are you…?" he started.

"Yes, I am the mother of Alison Bedoya."

"I am so sorry," he said, his eyes full of compassion. "She is not doing well. She has had several heart attacks. It is too much strain on her little body. I am so sorry. Your daughter will not return home."

I looked at the ground and saw my tears fall on the tiles beneath me. "Can I be with her?"

He nodded. "Yes, go be with your little one. Do you need to call her father?"

"She has no father…" my voice trailed off. "But can I call mine?" He handed me the phone.

My brother and his family had been visiting us in Quito, and my parents were at the airport dropping them off. My Dad answered his cell phone.

"Daddy," my voice cracked. "She's not going to make it." Those were the only words that made their way out of my mouth.

"We're on our way," he promised.

I hung up and was escorted into her room. There were several medical personnel in the room. They looked at me with pity written all over their faces. I knelt beside Alison's bed and held her hand. Her entire head was wrapped up in gauze all the way to her little nose. I couldn't see her eyes. I looked up at the nurse standing beside her bed. I asked, "Can she hear me?"

"Yes," replied the nurse. "If you want to talk to her, she can hear you." I know now that she was probably patronizing me. She probably did not think that Ali could really hear me. But I am so grateful that she gave me that hope, because I did talk to my daughter.

I stroked her little hand and sobbed. I told her over and over how much I loved her and how I needed her and I couldn't live without her. I told her that I had already wrapped her Christmas presents and that I needed her to come home for Christmas. I rubbed her little belly and ran my finger along her chin. I cried and cried. A doctor came in with a chair and helped me up in it. "Can I bring you anything? Perhaps a glass of water?" he asked.

"Fix my baby," I said. "That's what I need you to do."

"I'm so sorry, Ma'am" I thought back to the events that had happened the day before. I had awakened Ali before sunrise and dressed her. She had said goodbye to her Tias and we left for the hospital. We had waited so long for the day of her surgery to arrive. She had endured numerous appointments and procedures in preparation for this operation. I had prayed about this day for months. It was finally here and I was overjoyed. One of the top neurosurgeons in South America would be operating on her. An apparatus had been created specifically to be placed inside her skull to gradually close it. I knew she would never have a normal sized head, but at least she would be safe. I also knew her paralysis would not be healed, but she would be better.

We had picked up my mom at her house on the way to the hospital. The hospital where her surgery would take place was the most modern and most thoroughly equipped hospital in Ecuador. I had even heard someone refer to it as a five-star hospital. Upon our arrival, I was allowed to prepare her for her surgery. I placed her little white hospital gown with puppy dogs on her and tied it up. She modestly smoothed it down over her chubby little thighs. Then it was time for her to go into the operating room. I was allowed to wheel her on her gurney through the first double doors. When we approached the next set of double doors, I knew I would not be allowed to go further. Suddenly the nurse who was with me said, "Wait here a second. Let me make sure they are ready for her."

So I jumped up on the gurney next to Ali and I told her what was going to happen.

"They're going to take you in that room to watch some TV and then you're going to go night-night. When you wake up, Mommy will be right here. I love you so much my sweet little Preshy." The nurse did not return, so I continued to entertain my little girl. We sang the itsy bitsy spider and had a tickle war. About fifteen minutes later the nurse returned and announced it was time. I will be forever grateful for those fifteen minutes.

I leaned over my daughter and hugged her. "I'll be right here when you wake up," I promised again. Then I said goodbye.

She lifted up her little hand and said, "Bye Mommy." Then she blew me a kiss and I blew one back.

The surgery was expected to last six hours. I made sure the hospital staff had my cell phone, and I left. I returned about four hours later. My parents were taking advantage of their last day with my brother, and his family had asked me to call as soon as I knew something. I went to the nurse's station and asked for any information on the Bedoya child. No one could give me any details. I stood there feeling very alone. The minutes turned into hours. I paced the immaculate floors of the hospital. Where was my baby? Why had no one been able to give me any reports on her progress? I sat down in the black leather waiting room chairs and started writing in her journal. I stood up and sat down repeatedly. People around me could see my anxiousness. A lady sitting across from me asked, "Who are you waiting for honey?"

"My baby girl," I answered, forcing a smile, "How about you?"

"My son is also in surgery," she responded. We chatted a little longer to kill the time.

Soon, her 30-year old son was wheeled out and she jumped to her feet to join him. She didn't even turn to say goodbye. I paced some more. A friend of mine, Rolando joined me. He tried to keep me positive, but my stomach was in knots. As we talked, I suddenly bent over, clutching my abdomen and cried out.

"What's wrong Stacey?" he asked.

"I have no idea," I said. "I just got such a sharp pain in my stomach." I looked at my watch for the thousandth time. It had been exactly nine hours since I had last seen my daughter. That was three hours more than planned.

Soon my dad arrived. He had been waiting for me to call him and when I didn't, he decided to come anyway. He found Rolando and me in the hall.

"Still no word?" Dad asked.

I shook my head. "That can't be good can it?"

We stood there, the three of us trying to make small talk when suddenly the doors swung open, and I saw Ali's twisted little feet on the bed they were wheeling out. I ran to her, but they were going too fast.

"Stop!" I yelled. "That's my baby!"

Rolando ran with them, and I stayed with my dad to talk to Doctor Guerrero. He came out solemnly and explained the situation to us. They had known that Ali's skull was not complete and they were prepared for that. But in spite of all the CT- scans we had done, no one had ever realized that she had no brain sac. Her brain had been floating around her head. When they opened her skull, her brain spilled out on the table. The surgery took 12 hours instead of the expected six. They had done everything they could to patch her up. She had lost an incredible amount of blood and her body temperature had dropped dangerously low. They had rushed her to Intensive care because she had hypothermia and severe anemia. She had suffered a heart attack at exactly 5:00 p.m. I thought about how I had felt such a sharp pain at that specific time.

We went up to the ICU, but we were not allowed in to see her. Dr Pasternak, who had also been part of the surgical team, came out to explain things again to us. "She was a vegetable?" he questioned.

"Absolutely not," I said incredulously. "She speaks to me in English and Spanish. She knows her name and her caregivers' names. She calls me Mommy!"

Dr. Pasternak looked at my dad as if to say, "She's in denial isn't she?"

But my dad defended me. "No, it's true Doctor. She does all those things. That child is not a vegetable!"

"Well, then I hate to tell you that she will be now," he stated. "Parts of her brain have been handled and have been literally removed from her body and then put back. She will not be the child you just described. She may not recognize anyone or have any speech at all."

A chill ran across my entire body, and I sobbed into my hands. "Is she in pain?" I asked.

"No, she cannot feel a thing. When she wakes, however, she will be in excruciating pain. We will do everything in our power to help her deal with the pain. But it will be nearly unbearable for her."

I returned to the present moment as I looked at my little girl in front of me. I don't want her to ever feel excruciating pain, I thought. I laid my head down on her pillow and kissed her. "Oh Ali," I wept. "Please don't make me live without you. I'm positive that I can't. You have survived so much. You are so strong; I know that you can get through this too. Please, please Ali. I need you!"

Another doctor came in to inform me that my parents were in the hall. They were not permitted in the ICU. I went out to see them. I let myself fall into my dad's arms. I described how she was and told them the little that the doctors had told me. We walked around the hospital a bit. My parents seemed concerned that we should get back to ICU. Somehow, I wasn't as concerned. We prayed and we cried and then we headed back.

I asked my mom to please go to Precious Miracles to help with dinner and bath time for the other nine children. She selflessly complied. My dad stayed with me. He sat in the waiting room and I returned to Ali's bedside.

I grabbed her hand in mine and squeezed it. "Alison, I love you more than you could ever know. I had plans of us living the rest of our lives together. You are the best thing that has ever happened to me. I cannot bear to lose you."

Then I remembered her favorite song, the one I would sing to her at night before she fell asleep. And sitting there next to my precious little girl in the ICU, I sang.

Somewhere over the rainbow, way up high, there's a land that I heard of, once in a lullaby.

Somewhere over the rainbow, skies are blue. And the dreams that you dare to dream really do come true.

Someday I'll wish upon a star and wake up where the clouds are far behind me. Where troubles melt like lemon drops, way above the chimney tops that's where you'll find me.

Somewhere over the rainbow, bluebirds fly. If birds fly over the rainbow, why then oh why can't I? While I sang the song, Ali squeezed my fingers. I choked through until the end and then I kissed her cheek.

"Father," I prayed aloud. "I want my daughter here with me. I want her to wake up and be well. I want to see her smile again. I want to hear her voice again. But Lord, if you need to take my little girl to be with you, then Your will be done."

We were alone in the room. There were no voices, only the steady beeping noise coming from the heart monitor. I looked up at the machine. It was decreasing steadily. It went slower and slower until it stopped altogether. I raced into the hall just as a nurse was walking into our room.

"Her heart!" I cried. "I think it stopped!"

The nurse rushed in and then rushed right back out. Now there was no beeping, only panicked voices. In a wave of confusion, I was pushed out of the room and several staff members scrambled in. My dad saw that I had been pushed out of the room and came running to me. "What is it?" he asked nervously.

"I think she's gone," I answered. "Her heart beat stopped."

We stood there in the hall waiting. Dr. Pasternak came walking out of Ali's room. The look on his face told me what I was dreading to hear. When he got to us, he silently shook his head. I collapsed onto the hospital floor, sobbing.

"No!" I screamed. "No!"

The doctor and my dad picked me up off the floor. I thought about the prayer I had just prayed. I know God did not need my permission to take Alison to heaven. But I am eternally grateful that He did wait to take her until I had surrendered her to Him.

Ali lived the way we are all supposed to live. The fruit of the Spirit was abundantly obvious in her little life. She was full of love for others. She thoroughly enjoyed holding the tinier babies in her arms and feeding them their bottles. She reached out her arms to give a hug to anyone who looked like they could use one. She exuded unconditional love.

Joy was displayed in Ali's daily life, like no other child I've ever known. Ali's face seemed to be permanently fixed in a smile. She smiled at strangers and friends. When we were out in public, she was stared at constantly. But in her beautiful little mind she was convinced everyone that stared either thought she was strikingly beautiful, or else they wanted to be her friend. She would wave and smile at all the stares.

Ali had an almost palpable sense of peace. She comforted the other children when they cried. She had total peace about the way God had created her. One of the things that still breaks my heart to this day is the way Ali suffered in silence. I'll never know this side of heaven how much physical pain my baby girl was in. Some versions of the Bible call it patience, but in reference to Ali, I like to think of her as long-suffering. She was in pain, but no one ever knew because she was silent about it.

Kindness, goodness and gentleness were constant characteristics in Alison's treatment of the people in her life. She especially displayed them with the other children. She was sensitive to the needs of others. She was warm and caring.

Alison did not place importance in receiving things or getting her way. In her young three-year old body, she had already mastered the art of self-control.

My sweet, incomparable Alison was not impressed with a person's financial status or how many degrees they had obtained. She did not care if someone was poor and needy and uneducated. She had no conditions for the people she loved. She just wanted to be given attention. I could hold her and sing or read to her for hours, and she would be at her most content. On a daily basis, I saw the characteristics of Jesus revealed in my daughter. Her life motivates me to strive for authenticity and to continue to make a difference in the lives of the people God places around me. Everyone who knew my little girl is a better person for it.

27

three in one!

A tour of the Precious Miracles home was in progress when the phone rang. I excused myself to answer it. Melinda was on the other line. My previous experience had taught me that a phone call from Melinda usually meant one thing; there was a baby in need of a home.

Suspecting that I would know why she was calling, she casually said, "Hi Stacey, how are you?"

I grinned and said, "I'm okay what's new with you?"

"Well, I was wondering how many spots you have?"

I felt a stinging sensation in my chest as I was reminded that with Ali's passing six weeks ago, we had been left with one spot.

"I have room for one baby, Melinda, who is he or she?"

"Well, Stacey, the truth is, it's three. I have triplets."

"Triplets?" I screamed into the receiver. "Are you kidding me?"

Melinda quickly gave me the information. There was a woman at the maternity hospital in Quito who had delivered triplets twenty days earlier. The woman came from the province of Esmeraldas, on the border of Ecuador and Colombia. She was from a very primitive and remote community. Her village had no electricity and the river was their source of water. Her shaman father had determined she was carrying three babies, and she had come to the capital city to give birth to her children; one boy and two girls. The births had been relatively unproblematic, but the children were dangerously small. They were extremely underweight, and their health was fragile as a result. The doctors at the hospital refused to let her go home with her babies. The infants simply would not survive the lifestyle that awaited them. There would be no access to formula, and it was doubtful the mother could produce enough milk for all three babies. It would be impossible for their body temperatures to be regulated. And lastly, the trip in and of itself would be out of the question.

The hospital's social worker had asked Melinda if she would care for the newborns until they were stronger. Melinda's home was at full capacity, so she called me. I told her that I would get right back to her. I hung up the phone and went in to my office, shaking from head to foot. "Triplets?" I said out loud. That would bring our numbers up to 12. I didn't have three empty cribs. Where would they sleep? I rested my face in my hands and tears brimmed in my eyes as I prayed, "Please God, show me what to do."

My social worker, Veronica came in the office and seeing my tears asked, "Stacey what is it?"

I filled her in as quickly as I could. Then I looked to her and said, "I really want to do this. I want these babies in our home. But where will we put them? We have no cribs."

She smiled compassionately and said, "You have one crib, Stacey; Alison's."

I caught my breath and again felt tightness in my chest. That crib was almost sacred to me. It was Alison's. Was I ready to let another child, or in this case three, occupy it? Was I replacing Alison so soon? At these thoughts, the tears that had been struggling to stay under my lids spilled over and rolled down my face. And then, just like so many times before, I felt the peace of God envelop me. I heard Him say, "You have the room, the time, and the ability to care for these three children. I brought Ali home so that you could help these, my precious miracles."

I never tire of saying that God's peace truly does surpass all understanding. To the typical person without God, how can I explain that it made perfect sense to take in three children? I can't. But those who understand what it is to truly give something to Him and wait for His answer can understand that I knew that I was being called to care for these children.

And the peace of God, which surpasses all understanding, will guard your hearts and minds through Christ Jesus (Philippians 4:7).

I called Melinda back and asked if they could sleep in one crib.

"Oh Stacey, they are at about 2 pounds each! They could sleep in a bassinet together!" was her reply. "Does this mean you'll take them?" she asked excitedly.

"Yes," I answered confidently.

She said she could keep them for the night, and we made arrangements to pick them up the next morning.

If I had known how unusually little I would sleep in the days to come, I would have tried to rest more that evening. But the anticipation and excitement kept me up for most of the night.

The next morning, I strapped in three infant car seats in the back seat of my car, and with Veronica in the passenger seat, drove to For His Children. When we arrived and I saw the tiny babies lying next to each other in a crib, I was amazed by their miniature bodies.

How was it possible for a creature to survive being that small? How could everything in those tiny bodies be working? I had a momentary déjà vu, as I remembered three years earlier coming to this very place to pick up my very first baby.

It was December 2001. The paperwork to get Precious Miracles established had been stuck so many times, and I had been more frustrated than I had ever thought possible. I was renting an amazing house and had it very close to being furnished. I had cribs, bottles, tiny baby clothes, blankets, toys, everything except the babies. "Where are the babies?" I would cry at night as I stayed in this orphanage void of orphans. "You called me to this Lord! Why am I still waiting? Where are your Precious Miracles?" I would wring my hands with anticipation for the children that would fill the house with noise someday.

This one December morning, I had come up with a solution. I called my good friend Melinda who ran a home for children in north Quito. I proposed to her the idea of fostering one of her children. For all intents and purposes, the child she saw fit to give me would still be under the care of For His Children. I did not have the legal permission to take in children yet under my foundation's name. Instead, I would be a foster mom.

Melinda very kindly agreed that we could do this and arranged for me to have little Paula the very next day.

When I arrived at FHC that morning, she said, "We have little Paula, but we also have three preemies if you would prefer to care for one of them." As I looked at the three tiny infants, I got a little shaky. They were so fragile, so delicate. Would they break in my arms? I replied, as politely as I could muster up, "No I'm good with Paula."

That afternoon as I rocked Paula to sleep and thanked God for my first miracle, I also requested that He would please never send me any premature babies. "Lord," I prayed, "I don't know why I feel this way. I love children. I love babies. I want to serve you in caring for these your children. But oh Lord, I can't do the premature thing. They frighten me. Please, Dear God, don't ever send me preemies."

So now, here I am three years and one month later in January 2004, taking in not one premature infant, but three! I know God definitely has a sense of humor. I could picture Him in heaven saying, "Don't tell me who I can and can't send you! My grace is sufficient for you." And it definitely was!

We gently placed Maria Oia, Maria Pia and Juan Martin in their respective car seats and off we drove. Our first stop was at the pediatrician's office.

The last I had seen him was when I told him about Alison's death. He was astonished to see me walk into his office that day with a baby in each arm and Veronica following close behind with baby number three.

As Dr. Castillo examined the three miniscule children, it got strangely quiet in the room.

He looked up at me with a look that blended pain, compassion, and pity all together. He said to me, "Oh Stacey, what have you done? These babies should not have left the hospital yet. They aren't ready. You have three very sick and fragile little babies on your hands."

I tried to make sense of the words that were coming out of his mouth.

"What…What are you saying?"

"I wish I wasn't saying this, but I've always been honest and up front with you. They most likely won't make it… not all three! Are you ready to deal with death again…. So soon?"

I looked at him with disbelief. "Don't say that, doctor. Please don't say that. They WILL survive. I'll do the impossible to make sure these little guys make it."

He smiled and said, "That's the determination that characterizes your home, Stacey. I'll help in any way I can."

He gave me the rules in caring for children so small and weak. They were to be fed every two hours. They could not regulate their body temperature, so they could never be cold. I was to bathe them as fast as I could and get their clothes on and swaddle them immediately afterward. I was to keep them warm at all times. And lastly, they needed to be together as much as possible. They had just spent over eight months in very close quarters together. They needed each other.

I went home with my three babies and as I walked in the door, I said to the staff, "We have triplets. That's right, you heard correctly, triplets. They are weak and small and they really need me. In turn, I really need you to handle the other nine children." Having said that, I walked up the stairs to the spare bedroom where Alison's empty crib was being stored. For the next several weeks those three babies would become my life's purpose.

In those first weeks, the triplets proved to be by far the most difficult children I ever cared for. I followed the doctor's orders meticulously. I was determined to keep them alive. I would start feeding the one and then the next and then the last. By the time the last one finished her two ounce bottle, two hours had passed and it was time to start over with the first baby. It was exhausting.

Bath time also proved to be a challenge. I would fill the plastic tub with warm water and strip one baby down as fast as possible. I became quite the expert at speed-bathing and speed-dressing. After bathing three, I felt like I had gotten quite a workout. I put a space heater by the crib which remained on all night. At approximately noon every day, I could take them to the window and lay them in the sun's rays, wearing only a diaper for 15 minutes. When they slept, I would lay them side by side, their heads parallel with the side of the crib. If one was ever alone, he or she would cry until they felt their sibling next to them. It was truly remarkable.

Their mother came to visit shortly after their arrival at Precious Miracles.

"I don't know what I would have done," she commented, looking lovingly at her tiny children. "I have eight other children, but they all came one by one. I only have two breasts. I don't know how I would have fed them."

I chuckled as I put my arm around her shoulders. "I'm happy to help you out," I said.

"How long do you think you want the children to stay

with me?"

"I can't carry three children either," she said. "So, when they are eating normal food and when they are walking, I'll take them back." Spanish was her second language, and I asked her to explain their names to me. "In the Epera language, 'Pia' means precious and 'Oia' is happiness."

Because Pia and Oia were difficult to pronounce, we decided to translate the girls' names into Spanish. From that day on they were Preciosa and Felicidad. "And why does your son have a Spanish name?" I questioned.

"Juan Martin is the name my husband wanted to give the boy," she continued. "He needed a Spanish name because he will always have contact with the world outside of our community. My son is blessed you know. He will become the chief of our people one day because his birth was so rare and special."

The weeks passed and at their three month check-up, Dr. Castillo was in awe at their improvement. They had gained weight, they were alert, and they were no longer jaundice. The precarious hurdle had been overcome and their lives were no longer in danger. I was delighted to be able to get back into a routine with my other nine children.

Shortly after the babies had their first birthday, we began to consider the timing for their trip home. Juan Martin was walking completely unassisted. Felicidad was taking a few steps and Preciosa was on the verge. All three were healthy, strong, and chubby. They were also all eating solid foods. After some serious prayer and thoughtful consideration, the people involved in the decision all agreed the time had come.

The children's father came to Quito to complete the legal paperwork and to meet his children for the first time. His visit to the big city was certainly entertaining for me. He looked extremely uncomfortable in his long pants and long sleeved shirt. I'll never know who taught him to tie a tie. He walked awkwardly with the hindrance of shoes. I thought I was going to burst out laughing when I took him in the elevator to the lawyer's office.

His wide eyes looked all around him as the strange little box jolted us upward.

In Dr. Palacio's office, he was asked to sign several documents. He did not have a signature as he did not read or write. Dr. Palacio suggested that he leave his thumb print where the signature needed to go. With the legalities completed, he returned to his village and awaited the home coming of his children.

Flor Maria, the triplet's 16-year-old sister, came and stayed at Precious Miracles for a few days. We had decided that if they knew someone when they arrived 'home,' the transition would be easier. It was also helpful for her to see how we had cared for the children, their schedules and habits, etc.. Flor Maria returned home, and we prepared and made arrangements for the arduous trip to join her.

It seemed impossible as we discussed the logistics of this voyage. The nearest town to the indigenous Epera community is called Borbon. Borbon was six hours by car from our home in Quito. The car ride would be followed by a 30 minute canoe ride. The six hours in a car with three toddlers was daunting enough. I didn't even allow my brain to start thinking about the canoe. I packed three bags of things for the children. I packed a few warm weather outfits for each, a huge pack of disposable diapers, and their favorite toys.

The morning of our trip, we woke up the three dear babies and dressed them before the sunrise. Then I took a few minutes with each one. I brought them one by one into a quiet room and prayed with them. I explained to their groggy little faces what today was about to bring. We would be leaving Precious Miracles and everything that they knew, to embark on a life-changing journey. As I spoke these words to them, little did I know that the journey would be life changing for me as well.

On our trip, we had four adults accompanying the three babies; Ximena who had replaced Veronica as the social worker of Precious Miracles, Victoria, a missionary nun who knew the Epera language, and her friend Milly. There was no room in the car for three car seats. Milly drove, Victoria went in the passenger seat, and Ximena and I sat in the back with the three children. We had one carrier seat in between us and the babies traded off sitting in it during the trip. The six hour excursion turned into eight with our frequent stops. All three children got car sick, and coincidentally each one of them got sick while I was holding him or her. I was quite a sight, and my clothes were disgusting and foul when we arrived in Borbon. I couldn't get out of that car fast enough! The nuns in Borbon had prepared us a delicious meal and while the town was bustling around our three kids, we rested a minute and ate. After our meal, it was time to continue the journey to the village.

We managed to get all seven of us and the children's belongings into a canoe. Then, with three squirmy little babies we jetted down the river. It was all I could do to keep their little bodies inside the boat. As I looked into the disease infested water beneath us, I kept thinking to myself, "We're almost there. Just hang on! Stay with me and obey me for just a few more minutes."

After the longest 30 minutes of my life, we arrived in the village of the Epera Indians. The entire village was at the shore to greet us and, of course, meet the famous three children who they had heard so much about for over a year. We were helped out of the canoe, and we got a tour of where the children would live. It was a thatched roof hut, much like one would expect in the jungles of Ecuador. We had to climb an eight foot ladder to get up into the three room shack. Here, the triplets with their eight siblings and two parents would eat and sleep. Most other activities would not take place in the house.

At 5'7", I was unable to stand completely straight under

the ceiling. There were mattresses on the floor, and hammocks hanging from nails on the walls. There was a small wood burning stove and, of course, no electricity at all. There were a few plastic crates that had bananas and papayas in them. Magazine cut outs were stuck to the uneven boards that made up the walls. Across the top of the rooms were clothes lines where the few other items of clothing the family owned were being stored. A bright green parrot sat quietly on a twig in the corner.

As I looked around at this primitive environment, I had a lump in my throat. The American citizen part of me who was used to all her modern conveniences and luxuries thought, "nobody can actually live like this!" Then I swallowed deliberately and remembered that my mission with Precious Miracles was not to change all the indigenous cultures of Ecuador. Instead, I was called to help where I was needed and that is what I had done.

We dropped off the children's things on the boarded floors in one room and climbed down the ladder. As I stepped from one rung to the next I prayed, "Please Lord, keep my babies safe. They have never even climbed stairs before. This place is the farthest thing away from a baby-proofed house. Protect my sweet children."

We were escorted to the community hut a few feet away. This hut was closer to the ground and had virtually no walls. Mismatched boards lined the floor, and in the four corners were tree trunks that held up the woven branches that made up the roof. Pigs and chickens and monkeys were included on the guest list.

The people in the community were happily passing around the triplets who were surprisingly very cooperative with the whole affair. I saw Preciosa get a look of panic in her eyes. Then she caught the eye of her siblings, and I could literally see peace flood over her as her little shoulders relaxed and a grin spread across her lips. I too, felt peace at this moment. I knew that what was going to get them through this extreme change was going to be the presence of each other. They were so blessed to be three.

The people of the village had prepared a ceremony for us and they began with a beautiful dance. The babies were quickly included. Before long, someone had pulled me into the circle and I tried to keep up. They laughed, and I am quite certain I was being mocked. Following the dance, the President of the community got up to speak. She said in broken Spanish what a beautiful thing we had done for these children and how the Epera community was forever grateful and indebted to us. There was more music. A plate of miniature bananas was passed around. Then the father of the children got up to speak. His Spanish was lacking, so he requested the help of a translator. As long as I live, I will never forget his words.

"Out here in our Epera village, we have many gods. We worship the sun and we worship the snakes. But our sun and our snakes could not save my children's lives. Your God is bigger. Your God is the creator of the sun and the snakes, and your God has saved my babies' lives. We are forever grateful."

Because that which is known about God is evident to them. For since the creation of the world His invisible attributes, His eternal power and divine nature, have been clearly seen, being understood through what has been made, so that they are without excuse... Professing to be wise, they became fools and exchanged the glory of the incorruptible God for an image in the form of corruptible man and of birds and four footed animals and crawling creatures (Romans 1:19-20 & 22-23).

"I have nothing to give you that would ever repay you for the time, money and effort you put forth to keep my children alive," He continued. "I want to give my youngest daughter, Oia, your name. Today, Maria Oia is Stacey Michelle. And I want to give you the only material possession that I own." He turned around to a basket that was laying on the floor, reached in and pulled out a full-size hen. He picked her up and came toward me. I looked at him with alarm. I felt a surge of panic come across me as he laid that animal in my lap. "She lays eggs," he said with an enormous toothless smile. "She will be a good chicken for you."

I was as speechless as I have ever been. I held the restless bird in my lap and nodded repeatedly with my eyebrows raised as I said thank you. Ximena sitting beside me was trying unsuccessfully to stifle her laughter.

I feel compelled to write that we did take that bird back to Precious Miracles. She rode in the canoe, and then in the back of the car the entire six hours home. She did lay eggs and true to his words, she was in fact a good chicken for me.

When we returned home, the void the triplets left was almost palpable. Every other child had left Precious Miracles one by one. But here we were with three less children than we had two days earlier. I felt worried for their safety, and loneliness with their absence. But I rested in the knowledge that God had a purpose for bringing those three babies into my home and that He would continue to watch over them now that I could not.

I was blessed with the opportunity to visit the triplets several times. I was thrilled every time to see how quickly they had adapted to their own culture. As far as I can tell, they have no memory of warm baths with shampoo and baby wash in a tiled bathroom. The river seems to suit them just fine. They don't remember eating meals with silverware, fully clad with bibs around their neck and strapped into a high chair. They have no memory of wearing swim suits on swim days. Every day is swim day in the jungle, and why would one wear their clothes only to get them wet? They have no memory of flannel pajamas and clean sheets in their cribs every Friday. They have no memory of battery operated toys, the parrots and monkeys don't require batteries. What I first saw as a negative way of life was really only a different way of life. Who am I to say which way is the correct way to live? The Epera people are one of the happiest groups of people I have ever encountered. The triplets are blessed to call the jungle home.

Not that I speak in regard to need, for I have learned in whatever state I am, to be content: I know how to be abased, and I know how to abound. Everywhere and in all things I have learned both to be full and to be hungry, both to abound and to suffer need. I can do all things through Christ who strengthens me (Philippians 4:11-13).

28

paula

A Miracle says, "Thank You!"

Paula was contentedly buckled in the back seat of my car as I drove. She was on summer break from school, and I had taken her out for the day. We had gone to an amusement park and at her insistence, ridden everything they had to offer. For lunch, we had gone to a fast food restaurant and eaten junk that neither of us was in the habit of doing. We topped off our lunch with an ice-cream sundae. The activities of the day had no doubt worn her out, and she sat serenely looking out the window. I smiled nostalgically at the 5 ½ year-old little girl behind me. She had been in my care from when she was 10 days old until she was eight months old. At eight months, she had joined her adoptive family in Quito. That was also when I had transferred from being Mommy to Tia Stacey.

I began to reminisce about the time when Paula had lived with me. "How is it possible that one of the babies that stayed with me the shortest amount of time was also one of the children that had the most profound impact on my life?" I asked myself. Paula had been my first child. I had agreed to foster her for another orphanage before Precious Miracles had even been approved. I truly experienced single motherhood with Paula. I ate and slept when she allowed me to do so. If I needed to go somewhere, Paula came along. I did not have staff to give me a hand, so it had really been just the two of us.

Paula and I had bonded very deeply as a result of our situation.

Now here we were, five years later and still a part of each other's lives. We didn't see each other as often as I would have liked, but what a blessing to still get to observe her growing and thriving. My thoughts were interrupted when she said, "Where is little Sharon?"

Sharon had been at Precious Miracles the last time Paula had come to visit, and they had become fast friends. On today's visit, Paula had noticed Sharon was no longer living with me. I explained that Sharon had been adopted. "I was adopted," she said matter-of-factly. "I used to live in your house before I lived with my Mommy and Daddy."

"Yes, that's right!" I said with a smile, glancing back at her in the rear-view mirror.

She was quiet for a minute and then asked, "Did I come out of your belly?"

I reacted to the inquiry by putting my foot on the brake. I suppose that symbolically I wanted to put brakes on the conversation. "Well, no sweetie, you came out of a different lady's belly and then you came to live with me."

"Who was the other lady?" she asked.

I felt somewhat uncomfortable and out of place answering questions that maybe weren't my right to answer. But all the same, I felt obliged to calm her curiosity. "She was your birth mother," I explained.

"Why don't I live with her? Where is she?" she asked quickly.

"Your birth mother did not have enough money to buy your diapers and I did," I answered, in an attempt to think like a five-year old. "So I decided to take you into my home and buy you your diapers until God sent your permanent family that you live with now." She was silent as she looked out the window pensively, and I wondered if my explanation had helped or created more confusion.

"Was my birth mother pretty?" she asked, carefully pronouncing the words 'birth' and 'mother'.

My mind raced as I thought of how to answer this question. I didn't have the heart to tell her that I had never met her birth mother. Paula was one of the children who was merely discovered. She had been truly abandoned in every sense of the word. How could I explain that to her? In my opinion, she should never hear that part of her story.

But if she did, she should hear it from her parents, and it would have to be at a more mature age. So I simply answered, "Oh she most certainly was pretty, look at how beautiful you turned out!"

She smiled at the rationalization. She was silent for a long while before continuing, "Why didn't you keep me?"

"Oh Paula," I answered dramatically. "I cried so hard the day you left. I really, really, really wanted to keep you forever. But when God saw that I took good care of you, he sent me lots of other babies to take care of and our house got very full. If I had kept you, it would have been very difficult for me to be a good mommy to you and all the other children. Besides that, your mommy and daddy loved you so much, and they really needed a little baby in their house. God told me it would be better to let you go live with them, and I agreed."

"Did you need my crib and my bottles for the other babies?" she asked.

"Yes, I sure did. After you left, I used your clothes and blankets, your bottles and your toys for the other babies God sent me. Did you know that when Sharon came to my house she slept in your crib?"

"It's a good thing I wasn't still in it," she laughed as she spoke. "There wouldn't be room in that crib for both of us!"

I laughed too. By this time, we had pulled up to her house

and as I was unbuckling her safety belt. I said, "Did you have a good day today?"

"Yes!" she said excitedly. Then without any prompting she said, "Thank you Tia Stacey for taking me out today. And—thank you for taking care of me when I was a baby." And with that she flung her arms around my neck and squeezed.

If it had only been Paula, and I had not cared for any of the other 39, it would still have been worth it. And if I never receive another "Thank you" for the rest of my life, it would still be worth it.

epilogue

I wrote this book on my sabbatical from Precious Miracles. I had lived and worked in Ecuador for seven years without taking a furlough, and my emotional, spiritual, mental and even physical states were feeling the repercussions of that. Most of the children had left in adoption, and we had stopped getting phone calls to receive in more babies.

With the remaining children, I set up a foster care system. My good friends are helping me with the care of the children that remain under the foundation's custody.

Interestingly enough, some of the children are with For His Children, which is the organization that got me started seven years ago.

As I write this book, I have not yet had my thirtieth birthday. I ponder that fact, and am astounded. God has blessed me with an exceptionally rich, exciting, adventurous, and full life, and by society's standards I'm still young. It is overwhelming to consider how much more life I may have yet to live. I have been a foster mother to forty children; eighteen of whom had severe special needs. I started and administered my own foundation for seven years, and employed over thirty women. What will God do next? I have been through so many life-changing experiences, it is hard for me to fathom how my life could change any more. In the years at Precious Miracles, we fought numerous lawsuits, both personal as well as against the entire foundation. We received countless threats on our organization, most of which stated we were in danger of being closed down. I miraculously survived a near death car accident, was sexually assaulted, and being robbed on several occasions. I witnessed my mother being wrongfully incarcerated. I dealt with the pain and humiliation of a broken engagement. I endured the heart break of a failed adoption.

The Precious Miracles home was broken into, flooded, submerged in volcanic ash, and shaken by earthquakes. We repeatedly went days at a time without running water. The donations fluctuated dangerously at times, causing me to truly comprehend the term 'living by faith'. We had ten emergency room visits, eight surgeries, and more illnesses than I could ever list. I buried two children and said goodbye in one way or another to forty children who had become my reason for living.

> *And He said to me, "My grace is sufficient for you, for my strength is made perfect in weakness." Therefore most gladly I will rather boast in my infirmities, that the power of Christ may rest upon me. Therefore I take pleasure in infirmities, in reproaches, in needs, in persecutions, in distresses, for Christ's sake. For when I am weak, then I am strong (2 Corinthians 12:9-10).*

Of course, if you have reached this portion of the book, you already know it wasn't all pain and suffering. The blessings we received are far too numerous to count. Forty children's lives were positively affected by the work of the Precious Miracles Foundation. Children who would have died were rescued, families who needed a helping hand were given aid, and the most important thing of all, people who had never heard the name of Jesus are now on their way to heaven.

What will God do next? I can hardly wait to find out the answer to that question.

> *Now may the God of peace who brought up our Lord Jesus from the dead, the great Shepherd of the sheep, through the blood of the everlasting covenant, make you complete in every good work to do His will, working in you what is well pleasing in His sight, through Jesus Christ, to whom be glory forever and ever (Hebrews 13:20-21).*

Amen.